CROSSCURRENTS *Modern Critiques*

CROSSCURRENTS *Modern Critiques*
Harry T. Moore, *General Editor*

Frederick J. Hoffman

The Art of Southern Fiction

A STUDY OF
SOME MODERN NOVELISTS

WITH A PREFACE BY
Harry T. Moore

Carbondale and Edwardsville

SOUTHERN ILLINOIS UNIVERSITY PRESS

FEFFER & SIMONS, INC.

London and Amsterdam

To Elisabeth Holmes
who helped

Copyright © 1967 by Southern Illinois University Press
All rights reserved
Library of Congress Catalog Card Number 67–21039
Printed in the United States of America
Designed by Andor Braun

PREFACE

IT IS A PLEASURE to welcome another book by Frederick J. Hoffman to the Crosscurrents / Modern Critiques series. Mr. Hoffman, who is Professor of English at the University of Wisconsin at Milwaukee, earlier wrote for us a fine book on Samuel Beckett which was taken over by E. P. Dutton and Company for a paperback edition. Mr. Hoffman, author of Freudianism and the Literary Mind as well as various other distinguished contributions to modern criticism, is one of the most versatile of our critics and one of the most trenchant. Those who know his work will welcome the appearance of The Art of Southern Fiction.

Subtitled A Study of Some Modern Novelists, the book deals principally with writers who have come up in the "Southern Renaissance" which began in the 1920's. The South was once, recognized or not, a nation; its political boundaries were stamped out after the Civil War. But its cultural identity remained and, about two generations after Appomattox, began asserting itself in some of the finest literature that contemporary America has known, with William Faulkner, Robert Penn Warren, Eudora Welty, and other writers.

Mr. Hoffman, for good reasons, touches Faulkner only in passing, but he writes about Faulkner's important contemporaries. As Mr. Hoffman points out, Faulkner has been extensively treated elsewhere; one might mention (which he doesn't) Frederick J. Hoffman's own volume, William Faulkner, in the Twayne United States Authors

Series. But if Faulkner is not treated at length in the present book, it nevertheless contains references to him that are valuable, and it also provides some new perspectives on his milieu.

Mr. Hoffman's observations are continually valuable. In a chapter on James Agee and Flannery O'Connor, for example, he takes occasion to examine the religious values of the South. And he is consistently concerned with the "Southernness" of these writers, who have undergone what he calls the "indoctrination of place."

Besides dealing with the well-established authors, Mr. Hoffman explores a number of newer writers, including Reynolds Price and William Humphrey. He discusses not only their ideas but also their expressional abilities; he is not a critic who merely gives an account of what a writer is trying to say; he investigates the quality of the way in which it is said, so that he is always dealing, as a critic should, in literary evaluations. This is one of the things that help make Frederick J. Hoffman's books so good, and the present volume is a notable example of the method.

HARRY T. MOORE

Southern Illinois University
May 11, 1967

CONTENTS

INTRODUCTION

I SHALL WANT to be brief. There seems to me no need to explain, or to justify, the limits I have deliberately set upon the scope of this book. There are, of course, the alternatives of a two-hundred-page analysis of Carson McCullers' *The Ballad of the Sad Café* and a two-hundred-page "study" of a thousand novelists. Both of these are, of course, possible, and surely the latter is a task to be considered seriously (I should not want to be responsible for the former). In his *Renaissance in the South: A Critical History of the Literature, 1920–1960*, John M. Bradbury lists 524 novelists, plus hundreds of writers in other forms. He is an excellent critic and a careful historian; his book is indispensable. But there are two and one-half pages on Eudora Welty, four pages and eight lines on Katherine Anne Porter. *Verbum sap.*

The main purpose of this book is to put William Faulkner aside for a while and to give readers a chance to look at a few of his distinguished contemporaries or near-contemporaries. It is a commonplace of criticism (especially abroad) to speak of Faulkner and to close the matter of modern Southern Literature with a brief discussion or an extended discussion of his work. He is a worthy representative; one could do much worse than study him. But much very worthwhile literature is shunted aside as a result. So I have risked the experiment of bringing other writers to the foreground. Those who want many more names can consult John Bradbury's book. Those who wish to continue the Faulkner gambit may look into *William Faulkner: Three Decades of Criticism*, or (if they prefer the insights of one person) Mrs. Vickery's *The Novels of William Faulkner*.

FREDERICK J. HOFFMAN

The University of Wisconsin
Milwaukee, Wisconsin
August 25, 1966

The Art of Southern Fiction

A STUDY OF
SOME MODERN NOVELISTS

1 DEFINITIONS AND LIMITS

THERE IS, first of all, the matter of a definition: is there a fiction that is Southern? If there is, what boundaries may be set to it? If there is a place that can be discussed and marked, it must also have a history so that both time and place may conceivably play a role in identifying the literature. John M. Bradbury, in an Appendix to his very useful *Renaissance in the South*, lists some 524 Southern writers of fiction who have made some mark since 1920.[1] Bradbury's limits are interesting; they are chiefly a matter of geography and culture: a Southern author is one "who was born and has lived his formative years within this area." As for the area, it is a recognizably historical and cultural space, unified by a somewhat or moderately similar economic and historical growth. Bradbury excludes all Texans who are not close to the culture of "their trans-Mississippi neighbors," and he applies much the same rule to the state of Arkansas. As for the rest, he allows for a nice discrimination or two:

> Though I include Marylanders as dwellers below Mason and Dixon's line, natives of the District of Columbia can be allowed only in the special circumstance of family ties and interests. Washington belongs to everyone and to no one. (Marjorie Kinnan Rawlings, born in Washington, settling in Florida, and using the latter all but exclusively in her fictional settings, belongs to the South. A daughter of Calvin Coolidge born in the White House would not.) [2]

Bradbury's precisions are useful and acceptable enough. Having once settled for them, the question follows of what decisive identifying characteristics there are for Southern fiction. Robert B. Heilman, speaking of the "temper" of the South (a word that should include not only its literature but also its culture), defines that temper with a good sense of the scope and the particularity of Southern writing. "The Southern temper is marked by the coincidence of a sense of the concrete, a sense of the elemental, a sense of the ornamental, a sense of the representative, and a sense of totality." [3] While these qualities are shared by groups and areas other than in the South, their occurring together in one place and in one history is their distinguishing feature.

As for the first of these, the sense of the concrete, like many other critics Heilman associates it with the history of twentieth-century criticism; it may well be that the criticism, much of it connected with the *Fugitive* group in Nashville of the 1920's and the *Southern Review* group in Baton Rouge, 1935-42, is employed with the concrete aspects of literature.[4] The phrase applies also to the writing itself, as we shall see; Southern writing is a particularized vocation, preoccupied with images and words. There is less of the abstracting sense, generally, than exists in other literatures. While this statement may not appear to be applicable to such major writers as Faulkner, Robert Penn Warren, and Thomas Wolfe, I think it may be said that the more urgent of their assertions come strongly from their language and from the scenic treatment of human conditions in their Southern setting.

The "sense of the elemental" has to do mainly with the Southerner's preoccupation with first and last things; no one who has read much in the fiction will mistake the meaning of the next phrase, the sense of the ornamental—not, as Heilman admits, "superfluous or distracting embellishment," [5] but a sense of the incantatory powers of language, as well as a sense of its gifts of the grotesque and of the richness of the writer's powers. As for the "representative," it is a compromise between the abstract type and the welter of particulars from which it is difficult to draw lines of personal and group identity. Finally, the sense of totality suggests perhaps the richest yield of time and place: and awareness of the qualities residing (and coherently related) within a whole. We might say that tradition cautions us against the superficially temporal in life. C. Vann Woodward, a distinguished historian of the South, once said that "A Hemingway hero with a grandfather is inconceivable, and he is apparently quite as bereft of uncles, aunts, cousins, and in-laws, not to mention neighbors and poor relatives." [6] This is a remark, of course, that applies to Hemingway alone, but it is true that the intense preoccupation with the present is combined in his writing with an uneasiness in the presence of ceremony, ritual, symbolic suggestiveness, the kinds of ideational maneuvering that Hemingway once called "faking." [7] A mere preoccupation with the past and with its relations to custom and human ceremony may very well lead to a rather empty life, and there is enough of this attitude in Southern literature to suggest caution. But Heilman's use of the phrase is intelligent enough; it refers to the Southern writer's ability to go beyond the particulars of an experience and, without losing their concrete values, to use them in a wide-sweeping symbolic gesture or in a suggestion of the past's residing in and influencing the present.

There have been many other attempts to define and limit the subject.[8] I shall discuss some of the defining characteristics at some length and, I hope, in some depth, later in this chapter. I should like here to explore the significance of some remarks made in a panel discussion at Wesleyan College, Macon, Georgia, by writers in and of the South. The discussion was held on October 28, 1960; participating were Katherine Anne Porter, Flannery O'Connor, Caroline Gordon, and Madison Jones, as representative a group as we may hope to have together on one occasion.[9] There is the usual "how do you write" ploy, but the discussion is notable for another reason, the matter of concern for identity. This question is uppermost: in what way or ways do I qualify as a "Southern novelist"; how does my being Southern distinguish me from a Nebraska or a Wisconsin or a New York writer? A Southerner, said Miss Porter, "usually knows who he is and where he is and what he is doing," hence testifying to the value of an indoctrination of place (this despite the fact that she was herself the most restless wanderer of all modern Southerners). (p. 5) Caroline Gordon brought up one of the most frequently cited of reasons for identity:

> I think we have some awfully good Southern writers and I believe one reason they are so good is that we are a conquered people and we know some things that a person who is not a Southerner cannot envisage as happening. For him they never have happened. We know something he does not know. (p. 7)

This sense of self-awareness, what Miss Porter called "the tragic feeling about the South," is a mark of a distinctive difference. In terms of Heilman's phrase, "the sense of the concrete," it means that the Southern writer lives with an acute sense of human limit and limitation, and that he is aware of the human condition as specific, explicit, the bearing of the sinning and contrite personality. Miss Porter offered this version of the idea:

> Someone said that the resemblance of the real Southerner to the Frenchman was that we have no organized, impersonal abstract murder. That is, a good Southerner doesn't kill anybody he doesn't know. (p. 10)

There are, of course, many holes in the metaphor, but what Miss Porter intended to say is not hard to comprehend, and it may be wiser than most thrusts at the truth. She is a Catholic, as we know, and her sense of the Southern limitation is somehow associated with the qualities involved in the Christian condition of Grace. "I am sure that we are all naturally depraved but we are all naturally redeemable, too."

The idea, Calvin really put it into action, that God somehow rewarded spiritual virtue with material things, which
is to say that if you were living right God would reward you
with health and money, a good reputation, or the goods of
this world is to me an appalling doctrine. I happen to have
a faith that says the opposite, you see, that goods of this
world have nothing to do with your spiritual good and your
standing with God and I think that this attitude of the
South, when you [10] say they felt that if they had been right
God would not have permitted them to lose that war is
dreadful, you know. (p. 16) [11]

The truth is that the Southern attitude is compounded
of a sense of guilt, a feeling that there were a number of
"mistakes in the design," which led to defeat, and a sense
of the concrete limitation. There are two extremes, between which Southern literature is presented: The extreme of oratory and the extreme of the restricted image.
The one goes far beyond the elemental details of a given
condition (the monologues of Eugene Gant's father, in
Look Homeward, Angel, are a case in point [12]); the other
suggests generalities only in the way in which images
cohere and, together, hint at tradition (Eudora Welty's
Delta Wedding is an example [13]).

ii

Quite aside from the tug-and-pull of definitions
and analyses of Southernhood, there is the phenomenon
of literary eminence which remains to be accounted for.
From 1925 on,[14] Southern literature made a remarkable
impression, perhaps the most astonishing in the country of
our times. Just why this should be true is not altogether
easy to understand. If one were to look only superficially
at the scene and its history, he would think of many
reasons why it should not have happened: the South
suffered a crushing defeat in the Civil War; its lands and
industries were depressed for several decades, its people
impoverished; educational facilities were the lowest in the
country; the universities, for some years after the war,
existed almost in name only; tradition survived in a few

places, but was shattered elsewhere. A superficial inference from these conditions might be that nothing of enduring value could survive them, and nothing could be born.

But the opposing inference is also possible, and (as I have pointed out above) has often been made. Since the mid-1920's, Southern literature has grown rich in its abundance of gifted writers, and it has more and more compelled attention to its virtues. As the years advance, the writer and historian become aware of the variety and number of its stars; Faulkner seems at times to force attention solely to himself, and it has sometimes been difficult for newer writers to flourish in his shade.[15] Of course, the South has changed in other respects as well. At some time in its post-Civil War history it decided that the way to economic prosperity was to imitate Northern industrialism, to become "American" in the sense of showing evidence of economic superabundance.

The normal literary reaction to industrial progress is a literature of protest. The North has given us many writers whose work is nourished by the fund of satire, parody, irony, and plain realistic statement that such a situation provides. One of the most compelling literary products of the "blight of progress" was James Agee's *Let Us Now Praise Famous Men* (1941). But, as Agee says of it, it is not a book. "It is simply an effort to use words in such a way that they will tell as much as I want to . . ." [16] It is pre-eminently a work of talent and imagination, and it is perhaps a more powerful work than any ordinary work of social consciousness could possibly be. In the more traditional line of the "social novel," the South has had writers like T. S. Stribling, Erskine Caldwell, and Lillian Smith. This is, however, not the main line of Southern literature. The best writing goes deeper, sustains itself on other levels, exploits another vein.

Why should the region least favored by social and economic progress, suffering the worst damage to its institutions, prove to be the richest in literary gift, the most productive in works of more than passing interest? There is a complex of reasons, which may be generalized at some

risk of inaccuracy. It is true that the Southerner began in a
way of life different from that of the North. Even so, one
must distinguish between forms of legend and forms of
the actual. John Stewart has offered an interesting analysis
of the alternative merging and separating of these two
elements of the Southern past.

> Recognition of the two kinds, the legendary and the actual,
> and of the great diversity of the latter was one of the
> unavoidable and definitive moments in the artistic matur-
> ing of these writers. For some such as Faulkner and Miss
> Porter this recognition provided the ultimate source of
> many of their most intensely moving and meaningful fic-
> tions: untangling the threads of the actual from the galmor-
> ous fabrics of the legendary furnished them with story after
> story, while refurbishing the legend to serve as a means of
> binding up and giving shape and meaning to the pile of lint
> which was "what really happened" was the most difficult
> profound problem confronting them.[17]

It is this act of considering, staring at, brooding over the
past-as-legend, that dominates many of the scenes in
Southern fiction. It is, as Stewart says, extremely difficult
to distinguish between legend and actuality, and the gesture of trying to do so is in itself a major preoccupation in
Southern fiction. However the diversity of its expressions
in literature and of its realities, there was a "tradition," a
culture, based upon an economy, that was distinctive; this
tradition included a complement of ceremony, belief, and
dynastic observance. Those were forms of behavior that
were regionally distinctive. This is not to say (or, not to
say exactly) that the Southerner was more fortunately
born, but rather that he fancied he was, or that he exploited more fully than the Northerner the occasional
slight evidence of a leisurely, aristocratic world to which
he thought himself entitled at birth. The image of a
society graced by ceremony and by an affectation of culture took hold of the Southern imagination and was not
easily relinquished.

The South was also—and more self-consciously so than
the North—a *land,* more easily identifiable as such than

New England, for example, which was in essence an idea or a battleground of ideas.[18] The image of a land on which its people lived in close physical and moral dependency was a popular one and persisted in spite of all evidences to the contrary in the South's economic history. Here one must, however, call a pause, simply because two important changes have occurred in more recent examples of Southern literature: the shifting of scene from the land to the city, and the intellectual and moral change, from the Southern past to the contemporary universal. It may be that the writers who develop these two themes still possess a sense, however undeveloped, of the South as a place, a point of reference. Whatever the variants of belief, the idea of a land-as-a-whole, a cultural pattern, a *façon de vivre*, continued to be important in much of Southern fiction. From it arose several convictions, firmly held and hotly argued by many of the best Southern writers: that the land is sacred, that the really moral life is one lived in close relationship to it, that the land should not be "violated" (i.e., that Nature should neither be ignored, exploited, nor viewed abstractly), and that violation of the land is a major sin, for which there were major punishments. But the land was grossly abused in many ways. The defeat of the South in the Civil War was followed by the destruction of its pretensions to an agrarian culture. The "Agrarians" of Vanderbilt University in the 1920's and 1930's were all but in the act of defending a condition that existed only in retrospect. This does not mean that they were any the less sincere in affirming their position.[19]

But it is characteristic that Southern writers should both defend and represent a way of life at the point of its becoming scarcely operative. The literary record of the South's history since the Civil War is largely the history of a legend, the legend of a community and a way of life. The war threatened to destroy it, and in doing so made it more precious, more firmly a part of the aesthetic form that the legend retrospectively assumed.

Taking two of Heilman's phrases, the sense of totality and the sense of the concrete, I should like to suggest that the great value of modern Southern literature is derived from these two virtues. The "whole" that is in this connection imagined is not especially well associated with the real; it is for the most part the result of a refinement upon the crudest and rawest of generalizations. Southern rhetoric alters as it alteration finds, but one of its major functions is to make a half-truth whole, that is, to reveal its subrational nature, reveal it in as many of its human and natural ambiguities and paradoxes as the language can hold.

This rhetoric is also the style of the folk tale, the story told and retold, filled out by hazard and by guess, in the long afternoons and evenings of the Southern home, store, or public square. More than half of the literary forms that have excited modern readers have had their sources in this folk improvisation. The tradition of the folk tale is almost as old as the South itself. It has become sophisticated, or at least been made more complex, through generation into literary form. In the great folk-inspired literature of the modern South (Faulkner's *The Hamlet*, Carson McCullers' "The Ballad of the Sad Café," for example) the permanent truths of the human condition are given in a rich context of folk superstition, folk humor, folk pathos. The best writers transcend folk materials without too obviously showing their transcendence; the writings of Faulkner, of Robert Penn Warren, Eudora Welty, Carson McCullers, Caroline Gordon, Elizabeth Spencer, and others transmute the folk narrative into an examination of a universal moral circumstance.

Above all, Southern writing is noted for a sense of the concrete; the details that make the object "precious," that save it from annihilation by the abstracting mind, have nowhere been so much respected, so well understood. The individual scene, the fugitive nuance, the quality of tone of speech have been preserved. Perhaps the Southern literary tradition has been most active of all in adhering to the concrete fact. This is not often the "realistic" fact, or the scientific fact so much admired in most modern literature. It is the object, or the experience, observed with a most thorough and tender concern for preserving its essential nature. Quite aside from the debate over aesthetic and

formal concreteness,[20] modern Southern literature has preserved and utilized the natural folk lore of concrete detail,
in every aspect of public and domestic arrangement.
Much of this detail is violent, grotesque, the exaggeration
made palpably real. It is also clearly allied with the most
obvious and the most frequently discussed moral issues—the margin of error discernible in legal interpretations of man, the difference between Sunday display and
weekday decorum in the religious life, the special moral
issues arising from differences of temperament and race,
the inherited responsibilities and fates in family histories.

It is quite possible that the South has had the most
interesting and the most valuable literary history in recent
times because its writers have had more to go on, or more
to draw from. It suffered severely in the Civil War and
after it; its economic depressions and its political disgraces
led to a long period of reflection over human values, an
examination of the ideas, imagined or real or both, that
had gone into its social and moral structure. The pattern
of the Southern imagination begins in a world desirable
but not quite real, a product of the tensions of what John
L. Stewart calls the legendary and the actual; it proceeds
to a bitter struggle in which that world seems all but
destroyed; it becomes thereafter an ideal design of life
somehow vaguely located in a past (a pre-Civil War past);
and it is finally made to serve as a starting point for many
arresting examinations of the modern spirit.[21]

iii

I suppose that a reader may be misled by an
excess of enthusiasm into translating ordinary situations
and conditions into an elaborate *mystique*. Despite my
being aware of this temptation, as well as of the conflict
between the imaginary and the actual which is so clearly
the case in conditions like those which affect Southern
fiction, I should like to explore that fiction in terms of
place and time, and to risk certain elaborations upon both
terms in the course of identifying them with its history.[22]

There is some justice in the suggestion that much modern literature is a literature without place, one that does

not identify itself with a specific source. Partly this is a result of much exploration of universals, or of the fragments of universals. Human tensions are not necessarily associated with points on the map; in fact, they are often a consequence of the deprivation of place. Many crucial scenes in modern literature depend for their importance upon stereotype; details are not specifically related to geography but rather deny its function. The tendency is away from specificity, in the direction of archetypical resemblance. A scene occasionally suffers a loss of identity, as its spatial values become more and more isolated from cultural associations. Much of the psychic imbalance described in modern literature occurs in an abstracted setting; it is not identified with a place, a culture, or a family. There are objects, and they are spatially situated, but they do not suggest either a place or a history.[23]

The values of place in literature (as distinguished from *scene*, which is merely unindividualized space) come from its being fixed but also associated with neighboring spaces that share a history, some communicable tradition and idiom, according to which a personality can be identified. The interrelationship of personal and cultural history provides for a balance in human events that enhances meaning and locates it. Place is indispensable to scene in any literature that is more than merely abstract. Narrowly defined, a scene is merely a location in which certain things happen. The nature of objects arranged in a scene tells something about the quality of the acts; they depend indispensably upon their relation to place for any values that may exist beyond their distribution in space. The imagination is privileged to function in terms of scene, but in this role its opportunities are limited. It is only when a scene is identified with place that the full powers of the literary imagination can be challenged and used.

Eudora Welty has shrewdly defined the role of place in literature; its function is primarily to attach precise local values to feeling.

Place in fiction is the named, identified, concrete, exact and exacting, and therefore credible, gathering-spot of all that has been felt, is about to be experienced, in the novel's progress. Location pertains to feeling; feeling profoundly pertains to place; place in history partakes of feeling, as feeling about history partakes of place.[24]

These values are what precisely distinguish place from scene. It is really a question of types of knowledge and kinds of emotional commitment. In any truly successful literary experience, a place is endowed both with specificity of detail and a finely drawn line of association with time. The quality of a place inevitably derives from its existence in time; and as persons inhabit a place, they provide meaningful elaborations upon its intrinsic nature. Place may be called the present condition of a scene that is modified through its having been inhabited in time. The peculiarities of a scene are given it by such habitation; they are also the particulars of a scene, and when they suggest a shared experience, they move into patterns of history.

The great risks of the literary evocations of place are those taken in overstressing emotional values, of distorting their intrinsic qualities, or of isolating them from the geographical or historical patterns that help to contain them. An orderly progress from scene to place in literature involves a steady accretion of meanings; the particulars enlarge into generalities while retaining their identity as particulars. Thus a place metaphor is essentially a space image enlarged. Such a metaphor may be used—as Miss Welty uses it in A *Still Moment*—to suggest many implicit variants of meaning; it becomes a localized "morality image" in this case. The most successful developments of place in literature occur when the rhythms of time and generation are shrewdly and acutely used, to give a pattern or design to a place that its merely static detail scarcely suggests.

Places are redefined as *regions* when the characteristics of their geography and history maintain a surviving consistency of manner, despite local dissimilarities. This consistency is partly a matter of the weather; or, to put it another way, the weather helps to define a pattern of behavior, makes a manner of behaving possible or necessary. The rhythms of seasonal change, the relative persistence of degrees of heat or cold, the effect of long periods of either upon the density or thinness of the landscape—these are all determinants of a regional quality, to set off a place qualitatively from neighboring regions.

In *The Comedian As the Letter C* [25] Wallace Stevens has defined the extremes of North and South as excesses of order and excesses of natural abundance. In the one case, nature is sparse and intellectual mastery of it seems speciously easy; in the other, there is so great a profusion of natural objects that one is tempted to surrender to them, to give up trying to impose restraints. The implications for a social or regional way of life are obvious enough: where there are few natural objects, the mind moves quickly to impose an abstracting order; one is more likely, in a Southern landscape, to measure life close to the natural quality and pace of objects' growth. Thus order is more important in one kind of world, and natural lines of growth and being dominate in the other. One must account for objects where there are so many, and adjust to their peculiarities of growth and manner. One may generalize further, to suggest that a Southern landscape will perhaps have a more intimate history—that is, that it will account for many more particulars of being; and that, once a reasonable order of living is found, it will be valued more highly for its accommodation to life than for its demonstration of abstract principle.

The South as a region has these important distinguishing features: it is rich in natural detail; its pace is slow and close to the rhythms of natural sequences; it tends to develop historically in a slow accession of patterns which accommodate to the atmospheric and biological qualities of setting; it generates loyalties to place that are much more highly emotionally charged than is any dedication to ideas; finally, its rhythm of social motion is passive rather than active.[26] All these characteristics tend to encourage a conviction, one that gradually changes into a belief, that human processes and natural rhythms are closely associated and that the passing of time has in itself the generative function of shaping and solidifying tradition. Southern tradition tends therefore to remain static, to be self-protective, and to encourage fierce loyalties to its condition of being.

iv

This is perhaps the major reason why history plays so large a role in Southern literature. Even when there is no explicit reference to its history, the Southern character is assumed in terms of a regional history. The Civil War is of course crucial, but it is significant as a *defeat*, as a war—followed by a bitter thirty-year struggle against change—that forever fixed the value of a *status quo ante* and heightened the desirability of maintaining a devotion to what was imagined to be precious and inviolable. On one level, the Civil War enforced the Southerner's love of place by strengthening—perhaps even, in a sense, creating—platitudes of loyalty to it. Southern literature has frequently analyzed these clichés, chiefly in the description of mob violations of human proprieties. Beyond these, there is an abundance of place metaphors which, mainly in consequence of the psychological impact of defeat, emphasize the virtues of scene, atmosphere, climate, and landscape. The Southern scene is heavily charged with the task of communicating a special quality of atmosphere.

Far more important than any of these is the literary analysis of the South's psychological and symbolic inheritance. We may describe this as the "burden of the past." In large part, the errors and enormities of Reconstruction years are responsible for the overemphasis upon the Southerner's unique, independent, special fate and responsibility. As W. J. Cash has put it, the postwar Yankee failed dismally in his effort to change the Southerner's view of himself.

And so far from having reconstructed the Southern mind in the large and in its essential character, it was this Yankee's fate to have strengthened it almost beyond reckoning, and to have made it one of the most solidly established, one of the least *reconstructible* ever developed.[27]

Instead of forcing an awareness of a universal moral guilt, the Reconstructionist encouraged the Southerner to consider the moral "burden" of his past as a special problem, quite independent of a priori considerations of morality, a unique and a serious responsibility. The Southerner has reminded himself of his past, of its imagined glory and its inherited obligation. There is a great moral intensity in much of modern Southern literature, but it is neither the complex inner analysis that one sees in the New England literature of the nineteenth century nor the post-Calvinist rebelliousness of modern Midwestern writing. In many respects it suggests an attempt to purify the individual's sense of moral guilt by forcing an intolerable regional burden upon a single representative character.

It is perhaps unnecessary to say that this moral quality is not literary nostalgia. In Faulkner's analysis of the Southern mind, for example, he condemns as the worst of sins that of cultural stasis, symbolized in those "stubborn back-looking ghosts" that Quentin Compson imagines as he listens to Rosa Coldfield's recital of a hateful past (*Absalom, Absalom!*). Faulkner's brilliant analyses of the burden of the past emphasize again and again the risks of hardening any emotion with respect to history. They are at once a criticism of Southern truculence and of superficial Northern pieties.

It is impossible to speak of the South as place without discussing it as a region possessing a uniquely clear and responsible memory of its past. The psychological consequences of the Southern endurance in time have led to the use of the South as a pattern, an economy that has become a "way of life." Much is made in Southern literature of the ceremony of living and of the fact that living acquires certain habitudes if it persists evenly in time. A crucial theme in modern Southern literature is the contrast between the formal and the formless life. The man of boundless but empty energy, the directionless sensibility, seems to be either a Northerner or a "modern" phenomenon. The forms are derived from habits of family living through predictable generations, and from the symbolic values implicit in inherited and inheritable particulars. It is difficult at times to determine if the novelist wants us to believe in any one cause of breakdown; often, as in the figure of George Posey in Allen Tate's *The Fathers*,[28] it seems almost as though the collapse of forms were a matter of history itself, as though no traditional strength could have withstood the drive toward "modernity" and the loss of formal values consequent upon its arrival. Perhaps the interpretation suggested in Faulkner's works most adequately explains this condition. The untraditional man here forces a practical result outside time and tradition and thus violates all formal means of human containment. But Faulkner is remarkably *unhistorical* in his analysis of the past; his indictment of the moral evil in man is essentially an attack upon moral errors that occurred at the beginning of white Southern history.

Often in modern Southern literature the change from the "Old South" to modern times is dramatized in terms of a character who is unemotional, unattached, and amoral. The range of characterization is great, from Margaret Mitchell's Rhett Butler to Faulkner's Flem Snopes. *Gone With the Wind* is, in fact, the simplest and most superficial of historical equations; Butler, Scarlett O'Hara, and Ashley Wilkes provide the most obvious of speculations upon the weakness of the Southern historical metaphor. In each case—Faulkner, Tate, Miss Mitchell, Caroline Gordon—inner weakness conspires with external forces to threaten the center of the metaphor. Nevertheless, the place metaphor persists as a symbol of a value regionally preserved. It is always a place in which—as a consequence of nature's bounty, human strength and persistence, and a strong sense of loyalty to tradition— humanity is a concern, and its formal, even ceremonial, values are treasured. Implicitly at least, often quite openly, this metaphor is threatened by an inhuman, impersonal agent which exploits and destroys nature without love of it or respect for the ceremonies of man's living with it. Faulkner speaks powerfully against these forces, nowhere more vehemently than in "The Bear," where he describes the "doomed wilderness whose edges were being constantly and punily gnawed at by men with plows and axes who feared it because it was wilderness . . ." [29]

v

Substantially, the moral implications of these several examples are related to the problem of using space. Once again it is a question of the difference between Northern sparseness and Southern abundance of natural imagery. Those Southern novels which speak historically of the move westward (Caroline Gordon's *Green Centuries* and Elizabeth Madox Roberts' *The Great Meadow,* among them) describe the lure of rich lands, exploited and ready for human habitation. But the moral relationship of man to nature is also closely emphasized here. The figure of Daniel Boone serves both Miss Gordon's and Miss Roberts' novels as a symbol of human discretion and an unspoken code of manners. Part One of *Green Centuries* has as its epigraph this statement of Boone's: "I think it time to remove when I can no longer fall a tree for fuel so that its top will lie within a few yards of my cabin." Miss Gordon's historical novels define the progress of a fine balance of man and nature—the gradual and natural evolution of families, houses, estates, and communities. In this case, the place has achieved its status as metaphor in the literature of the South by a finely balanced movement into and through nature, which is not a "temple" so much as a dwelling place.

This metaphor—of the land as a place on which one may respectfully and sensibly live—is linked to the power of the human mind, an outward expression of self-identity. This metaphor strongly informs the writings of Elizabeth Madox Roberts. For the heroine of *The Great Meadow* the acts of life and the rhythms of nature had instinctively sought out and achieved a rapport, which is central to her conception of place.

The curing of the meat filled the late autumn, work going forward all day in the frosty air, and the wind washed over their bodies in a fine subtle spray. For many weeks none had come from the outside. The dusk would fall and the nights were long. There were long evenings by the fireside in the new house.[30]

History is here seen as a manner in which men contain themselves, within a necessary, functional architecture and routine. Similarly, Ellen Chesser in the fine novel, *The Time of Man*, endures all human vicissitudes in the confidence that she is situated in space and that there is a place for her uniquely within it:

There a deep sense of eternal and changeless well-being suffused the dark, a great quiet structure reported of itself, and sometimes out of this wide edifice, harmonious and many-winged, floating back into blessed vapors, released from all need or obligation to visible form, a sweet quiet voice would arise, leisured and backward-floating, saying with all finality, "Here I am." [31]

The history of the Southern place is essentially one of human agreements made with nature. Miss Roberts' heroines are often too awkwardly and too easily moved by a backwoods idealism, though she atones for these excesses by her careful and precise portrayal of folk identities. Throughout the Southern literary evocations of the Southern past, this metaphor of a place inhabited, worked, and loved, dominates. Its opposite is the place destroyed, ignored, or laid waste. The evil of man's acts is most frequently described in terms of the destruction of place images—or, as in Faulkner's *Intruder in the Dust*, the construction of places not worthy of their setting. Sometimes the decline of the human world is shown in terms of the reduction of the space itself. The very complex space metaphor of Faulkner's *The Sound and the Fury* describes for us a steady diminishing of the Compson world during the thirty years of the novel, until in Part Four one really sees only the kitchen of the house where the only fully living person, Dilsey, works. The very intense moral judgment is seen at work in other Southern novels as well. The disastrous collapse of human dignity is described in William Styron's *Lie Down in Darkness*, in a series of images in which space values have been all but eliminated. Peyton Loftis, whose suicide reminds us in some ways of Quentin Compson's, is first inadvertently buried in Potter's Field off Manhattan; then her body is rescued and shipped to her father's home in Virginia, the survivors suffering one agony after another on the funeral journey. The ignominy of death repeats the indignity of her life.[32]

The importance of place in Southern literature begins with the image, the particular of the Southern scene, a quality of atmosphere or a simple human detail. Its specific Southern quality may be simply an eccentricity of genre; it may be and frequently is a detail of idiom or manner which used to be labeled "local color." Place builds out from it; it is made up of a cluster, or a mosaic, or an integrated succession, of images. The significance of place argues some accepted history or co-ordinated memory which is attacked, defended, or maligned (it is never ignored, or merely set aside). History within an established set of spatial circumstances moves easily into local culture, or tradition. Relationships of class or race or peoples have their own ways of modifying memory or adjusting to historical change.

The most eloquent of Southern "place" fictions are quite clearly fixed in "pure" images of setting. They begin there, but they don't remain there. How they begin, and with what precision of meaning they will ultimately be used, is a matter of the knowledge and love of place. As Miss Welty has said, the quality of a described place is an index of the precision of feeling. Her work is a remarkable testimony of the literary significance of place. Much more than Miss Mitchell's Georgia (which never stands still) or Mrs. Rawlings' Florida (which rarely moves), her Delta country clearly establishes its meaning in the rich detail which is its substance. The detail affronts the senses from the very beginning; in *Delta Wedding*, as Laura approaches the community of Fairchilds, Miss Welty says,

"The land was perfectly flat and level but it shimmered like the wing of a lighted dragonfly. It seemed strummed, as though it were an instrument and something had touched it." [33] The landscape quickly assumes a particular quality; it "fills in." There is a succession of images, with or without personal reference, each of them adding some minor poetic quality to the scene. Before the day has concluded, the scene has become a place, the place has acquired a character, the character, an implicit history. It is a remarkably unified place; everybody "was kin." Both the strength and weakness of Fairchilds rest upon that fact, and the conflict that builds the narration is a commentary upon it.

Delta Wedding is a superb illustration of literary sensibility informing place, and being informed by it. The progress is in terms of discrete entities, which yield slowly to formal orders and ultimately give way to a major commentary upon certain universal human qualities. Miss Welty has fully realized her "place"—as, in quite a different sense, Faulkner "realizes" the area not too far to the north of it; as, indeed, Thomas Wolfe vividly represents the Asheville of his youth, at least in *Look Homeward, Angel*. Certain special qualities of place are sometimes developed thematically, to some advantage. The mountains that "rimmed" Altamont acquire a special value in the economy of Eugene Gant's romantic disposition; they come eventually to symbolize the containment of what Wolfe calls "the core and desire of dark romanticism." They do not contain so much as frustrate, and the degree of frustration is marked by the excesses of what Eugene's parents do to adjust to their separate conditions.

More specifically, the heat is made an atmospheric quality of the Southern place. It is always present, even if momentarily it may not exist. It is to be endured, but it also often takes over, to dominate the meaning of a place. The atmosphere of Faulkner's "long summer" mingles with the sound of the cotton gin, to create but one melancholy effect.

It was now the third week in September; the dry, dust-laden air vibrated steadily to the rapid beat of the engine,

though so close were the steam and the air in temperature
that no exhaust was visible but merely a thin feverish
shimmer of mirage.[34]

In this heat-laden world Faulkner plays out the mock idyll
of Ike Snopes and the Houston cow. Frequently the heat
atmospherically deceives, as in Lena Grove's slow progress
along the road to Jefferson in the beginning of *Light in
August*, until suddenly one realizes that it has hung over a
setting of violence.

These particulars are not in themselves especially significant of place; it is what they ultimately do, by providing
either an incidental *décor* or a thematic substance, that is
important. In the end, it is not the heat or the color or the
lines of terrain in *Delta Wedding* that are significant, but
what they cumulatively and ultimately make of the images
of the two houses at Fairchilds: Shellmound, where life
flourishes, and Marmion, where it has scarcely entered.
Such details—odors, colors, temperatures—play the imag-
istic supplementary role in Faulkner's *Absalom, Absalom!* They define the moral economy according to which
Quentin is finally to appraise the story of Thomas Sutpen
and to determine what his attitude toward it will be.
Throughout this novel, as well as in Part Two of *The
Sound and the Fury*, the nature of his self-judgment is
given in terms of atmospheric clashes: the iron, cold New
England room clashes with the hot, pine-winy, heavily
scented Yoknapatawpha world, bringing him closer to his
own act of violent resolution.

There are many Southern novels which offer an abundance of scenic detail, but do not, for all that, use the
scene to any great purpose, and often the knowledge of
region has to stand almost by and for itself. Marjorie
Kinnan Rawlings' Florida "scrub country," for example, is
fully evoked in *Cross Creek*, and in such novels as *South
Moon Under, Golden Apples,* and *The Yearling*. The last,
a great popular success, is an excellent example of a literature full of atmospheric detail, much of it convincing and
instructive; but it tells a story that is painfully slight and
trivial. There is no question of Mrs. Rawlings' success in

communicating the surface of the place: the difficult, all-but-primitive wilderness, the impact of the weather (calamities of both drouth and rain), the struggle to make a livelihood in the face of extraordinary obstacles and misadventures. All of this convinces the reader that he "has been there," but he is also asked to accept a narrative line which—except when it pauses within the scene itself—is childish and superficial.

Du Bose Heyward's fiction is of a quite different quality; two of his novels, *Porgy* and *Mamba's Daughters*, make the most of "local color" by portraying Negro life, habit, manner, and speech. However, this raises the risk of allowing the "quaintness" of dialect and behavior to dominate and to put the reader in the uncomfortable position of condescending to the novels almost from the start. There is no doubt from the evidence of his books that Heyward knows his characters in the idiomatic sense; they are "folk" whose rhythms and mannerisms he had experienced at firsthand. The Charleston Negro life in *Porgy* testifies again and again to a surface accuracy and honesty. Nevertheless, there is reason for feeling that the tragedy of the crippled Porgy is a "play-acting" event; one almost feels that the novel deliberately anticipated the play Heyward and his wife adapted from it, perhaps even Gershwin's opera, *Porgy and Bess*.

As a novelist, Heyward is too much the white-man master of ceremonies. The tone of his introductions is slick and artificial; as a result, the qualities of character and dialogue come almost as a surprise; the reader is scarcely ever more than a man in an audience, having the particulars of a scene pointed out to him by a man who has learned his lines and the appropriate folk accents. "In those days," he says by way of introducing Porgy, the profession of beggary "was one with a tradition. A man begged, presumably, because he was hungry, much as a man of more energetic temperament became a stevedore from the same cause." The same quality shows in the passages of dialogue, which in itself has a richly phonetic flavor:

". . . Yas; my belly fair ache wid dis Noo Yo'k talk. De fus t'ing dat dem nigger fuhgit is dat dem is nigger. Den deh comes tuh dese decent country mens and fills um full ob talk wut put money in de funeral ondehtakuh pocket." Breathless, she closed her arraignment by bringing a fist the size of a ham down upon the table with such force that her victim leapt from his chair and extended an ingratiating hand toward her.[35]

Hamilton Basso's chronicling of Southern manners bears some resemblance to J. P. Marquand's portrayal of the New England social manner. Frequently the Basso hero is an "intellectual"—a scientist, a professional man, a journalist—who is handicapped by inherited prejudice, economic circumstance, or other difficulties in his effort to achieve self-knowledge or a proper situation in life.

The View from Pompey's Head is Basso's most typical use of the Southern theme; it is at once his most popular and his best book. He "gets at" his subject in a fairly conventional way: an "exiled" Southerner, who had gone to New York for his career, returns on assignment from his law office to the home of his youth and his past. Basso has him work not only for the completion of his mission but, more important, for the clues to his love of the South and the undercurrent of attachment he has always had for the region. Basso neither entirely attacks nor altogether defends the South; he is primarily concerned with setting its virtues against its weaknesses, and the latter are primarily associated with a false pride of ancestry (Southern Shintoism, as the hero had once labeled it).

The novel maneuvers easily through its details of place, heritage, and mannerism. It is "liberal-ethical" in its moral position with respect to the South, and combines a critical with a nostalgic sentiment toward the South Atlantic town of Pompey's Head as a symbol of the South. In his position as rational analyst of the Southern view, the hero, Anson Page, describes its "trouble" as the sentimental image of a landscape: "It's a kind of never-never land, everything, everything about it—the moss in the trees, the way the sun sets, the haze on the river and those fogs we get just before dawn . . . it's not real, only there it's real, and so the true reality is somehow lost and nothing seems improbable but the world as it actually is." [36]

This book and, in another way, its successor, though not its sequel, *The Light Infantry Ball*, gives a panoramic view of both space and time; it muses editorially over human passions in a Southern setting. It is slick and rather agreeably obvious in its narrative line (one can easily imagine its having been run as a serial publication); but there is little beyond this surface impression. Neither the characters nor the scene gives more than a two-dimensional effect.

The Yearling, *Porgy*, and *The View from Pompey's Head* illustrate the popular exploitation of the Southern scene. As impressions of that scene, they do not conspicuously succeed: the Negro dialect (painstakingly ever-present) of Heyward's *Porgy*; the rather thin line of narrative concern with juvenile brooding over the maturing of animals in Mrs. Rawlings' *The Yearling*; the rather arbitrary plot strategies of Hamilton Basso's *The View from Pompey's Head*. While they are "South," they scarcely communicate except to a touristic interest in regional differences. When the images of place convincingly group, to suggest ideas and moral substance, when they exist both on the level of independent objects and in terms of a history or a tradition or even a memory of men related to a quality of place in generations of time, they contribute to a literature of place. The intensity of the moral vision that informs them, in terms of a succession of significant human disasters makes them valuable. Above all, the *sense* of place, which is associated with a reading of the human destiny, defines precisely the meaning, at both the beginning and the conclusion of moral reflection.

Allen Tate, speaking of Emily Dickinson's poetry, finds in it "a tension between abstraction and sensation, in which the two elements may be, of course, distinguished logically, but not really." [37] He is, of course, applauding her sense of personal involvement with "ideas," but it is above all the clarity of image that charms and not the awesome importance of the idea. In literature, ideas help to define and direct emotions, which have the specific value and quality of their situational and historical conditions. They are thus transmuted into images large and small, varied and simple, which endure, to which loyalties, responsibilities, "burdens" are attached. These literary growths become the cultural history of place.

The "lesson" Katherine Anne Porter's Miranda learns in *Pale Horse, Pale Rider* points up the readjustments to place necessary from generation to generation. She at first acknowledges place and tradition in terms of souvenirs treasured by her grandmother. The past is threatened by evidences of its decay; Miranda is disabused of the past's value by the presence of near-ghosts. Yet, in a revised context, tradition is resumed in her. The keepsakes of her grandmother's world are revivified (even though, *as objects*, they are destroyed) as they pass through time. The ceaseless struggle of a place against the threat of its being contained and made absolutely static by an obsessive memory is an important part of the dynamics of place literature. Time fixations are an influential aspect of both Northern and Southern literature; one need only remember the several frightening objects of the past which destroy the present in O'Neill's *Mourning Becomes Electra* to realize that this is so. No more devastating Southern counterparts need be indicated than Faulkner's *A Rose for Emily* and Warren's *The Circus in the Attic*. The most vividly concrete particular can become the worst kind of abstraction if it is allowed to work erosively upon the present. That is why the most successful of place literature is that which presents its details as freshly and intimately renewable. In the finest work of Eudora Welty—notably, *Delta Wedding* and the superb book, *The Golden Apples*—the minutiae of place are vividly clear and precise, even at the moment of their dying, because of the promise of and the provision for their imaginative renewal. But one must remember that truly evocative place literature like Miss Welty's gives us more than a reiterative idiom or more "local color"; these last are more of antiquarian than literary interest.

The literature of Southern place belongs in three major classes: that which defines, describes, and preserves the tradition without abstracting it (Miss Roberts, Caroline Gordon, Ellen Glasgow); that which reveals the genuinely native particulars of a scene, while at the same time communicating their existence in time and commenting on it (Miss Welty, Shirley Ann Grau, Carson McCullers, Flannery O'Connor); and that which explores the complex inward influence of place as moral "fable," directing or at the least influencing the rhetoric and the pace, and ultimately serving a decisive role in the novel's substantial meaning (Faulkner, Wolfe, Warren).

I WISH TO DISCUSS a select group of Southern novelists in
this chapter, writers who have worked both with modern
and with traditional matters affecting the South. It is not
so much a matter of generations, though most of these
writers antedate, by a few years or more, those treated in
later chapters. They have, pre-eminently, established what
may be called the tradition of the modern. Part of that
tradition is a fictional representation of the South (or a
part of it) since the end of the Civil War and the time of
the Reconstruction. Though Ellen Glasgow (1874–1945)
did precisely that for her state of Virginia, her fiction
describes an earlier generation (her first novel *The Descendant*, appeared in 1897). Since I wish to put most
weight upon the generations of Eudora Welty (born
1909) and of William Styron (born 1925), Miss Glasgow
belongs to an earlier time, and besides she has been gener-
ously studied already.[1]

Much the same may be said of Elizabeth Madox Roberts (1885–1941), whose first publication, a book of
poems, was published in 1915. Her work was grounded in
the Agrarian heritage, to which was added both an historical sense and an intimate sense of the folk. As Harry M.
Campbell and Ruel E. Foster have said, "there was a
feeling for place, for state, for the 'Kentuckyness' of her
life which was an integral part of her life, important in her
art, and which never diminished."[2] *The Great Meadow*
(1930) is in many aspects a basis text in the history of

Southern backgrounds, and it as well offers something of a metaphysical source of the pioneering, westering soul of the nineteenth century:

> She [Diony] would return to the words of the book and heed what they said, in substance: that all knowledge is of three sorts, that derived by way of the senses, that by way of the passions, and lastly, quoting now the words of the text, "ideas formed by help of memory and imagination." [3]

The Great Meadow is demonstrably a novel about the pioneering, westward push, and Miss Roberts brilliantly handles both the most explicit details and the broadest of explanations. There are many impressive touches in the novel, but it may be that interest in it depends too much upon the provincial detail. Miss Roberts has few peers in the matter of communicating the reality of history. *The Time of Man* (1926), while it was originally the more successful book, is less able to hold up under the demands of rereading. Yet, it is the work of an interesting mind and of a solicitous imagination. The imagination settles upon Ellen Chesser, a descendant of Kentucky pioneers, a poor white, a woman of tremendous interest despite her lack of sophistication.

Both Miss Glasgow and Miss Roberts depend upon the tradition (they sometimes write "historical" novels), without offering an essential *theory* according to which the tradition may be comprehended and discussed at length. There is a feminine concern with the kitchen, the pantry, and the bedroom, as fixed centers of human interest, and the masculine impetus to westward movement is seen in a kind of telescopic view.[4] The perspective is admirable, but it needs to be supplemented in order that the full complex of Southern history and tradition be appreciated. Whether it deserves to be or not, the so-called "Agrarian" movement in modern criticism and economics proves to be central to speculations upon the Southern tradition and its points of distinction and difference. The history of the Agrarians is not my concern; it has been given in about as many good studies as any comparable development in modern literature.[5]

Robert Penn Warren, however, occupies an almost unique position in this context. He was, belatedly, a member of the original *Fugitive* group, having joined it in 1923; he contributed an essay, "The Briar Patch," to *I'll Take My Stand*,[6] whose publication in 1930 was one of those cultural landmarks that will be exploited forever by historians and journalists; most important, he was a man of great talent, whose poetry and fiction have since 1936 illuminated the Southern landscape.[7] John L. Stewart has suggested the central fable of both: "For more than twenty years Robert Penn Warren has been engaged in telling successively more elaborate versions of the same story—the story of man's effort to flee from the problem of evil and of his ultimate return to that problem." [8] The encounter with evil is in Warren's representation if it akin to confrontation with the natural world; man must learn to live with evil as well as he can. The condition of the Warren hero is that of Adam after his departure from Eden. The Adamic knowledge, therefore, involves an experience within the post-lapsarian world. It is true that his characters sometimes try stubbornly to stay in Eden; the name Adam Stanton of *All the King's Men* (1946) suggests an important example.

But man must enter the world; all of the moral complexities of his tenure on this earth work out from his having resisted the life of the "peaceful stone." Man is a violent creature, and the violence is part of his move toward awareness. The richest source of literary virtues comes from certain basic uncertainties most of Warren's narrators possess; they are conscious of a desirable end and of certain steps they need to take. But their course in life is otherwise filled by half-definitions, tensions, and rationalizations. Man is worthless if he does not take his chances in the world. He looks back, wishes himself back, in the womb of circumstance:

If I could pluck
Out of the dark that whirled
Over the hoarse pine over the rock
Out of the mist that furled
Could I stretch forth like God the hand and gather

For you my mother
If I could pluck
Against the dry essential of tomorrow
To lay upon the breast that gave me suck
Out of the dark the dark and swollen orchid of this sorrow.[9]

This fundamental necessity, indicated in the syntax of these lines, lies in the confrontation of evil; it is a part also of the "Agrarian" argument against the sure certainties of the scientist; John Crowe Ransom's *God Without Thunder* (1930) is an important document in that history.[10] The poetry of Warren balances well against the fiction, to elaborate upon these themes and experiences. "The Ballad of Billie Potts" has many of the conflicts and tensions that Warren dramatizes in his novels (*Selected Poems*, pp. 3–17). It is a "cross-purposes" fable, rich in folk ironies. The westward move, present here and in the fiction, is an especially complex metaphor; as Stewart says, "Driven by some great nameless force, the pioneers move westward, always longing for the lost innocence of the childhood of the race as the modern man flees into abstraction in search of the lost innocence of childhood." (*South Atlantic Quarterly*, p. 572) Warren seems to be saying that a new kind of innocence is necessary, the innocence of Adam beyond the Garden, of the acceptance of guilt.[11]

This, then, is the pattern, as it relates to Warren's fiction:

1.   The beginnings are in innocence, in the form of an immaturity or an incompleteness.

2.   The world is next in the sequence, and the person facing the world: the world is a place of particulars, and man must find a "path of action" that will test his principles, whatever these may be.

3.   Man, entering the world, can commit one of two kinds of sin (or both of them): he can violate the particulars of the world in order to achieve power;[12] or he commits acts of violence on the assumption that they are "principled" acts. Warren's characters suffer from the complex web of human fate, but their experience is indispensable to their self-awareness.

In the first novel, *Night Rider* (1939), based upon Warren's investigation of the tobacco war in Kentucky, 1905–8, Percy Munn is established as the hero who must work through experience to a redefinition of awareness. Here, man changes gradually from a person identified with the land, to an abstract, violent being, who ends by committing acts without really knowing his motive for them, or even their nature. Munn's mistake is his attempt to "find himself" in mass action and in violence. The entire personality of Munn changes. As he becomes involved in the organization, he is less and less able to communicate with his fellow humans.

At Heaven's Gate (1943) has a more explicitly modern setting, but the theme is not dissimilar from that of *Night Rider*. Against the apparently directionless careers of the majority of the characters, Warren presents the Ashby Wyndham story, which suggests a form of "salvation" in a world otherwise almost empty of moral and religious meaning. In *World Enough and Time* (1950), based on an actual anecdote, which was described in *The Confession of Jeroboam O. Beauchamp*, the hero (Jeremiah Beaumont) in his search for truth invents a myth about himself. The novel is rich in both human and physical circumstance, a truly "luxuriant" Warren novel. Beaumont encounters violence, commits it himself, attempts to escape by moving westward, but finally returns, to accept the consequences of his acts.

Perhaps the Warren pattern is best seen in *All the King's Men* (1946).[13] Warren had first written a play, called *Proud Flesh*, on the subject.[14] The novel itself is richly textured, and it introduces several groups of characters in a much more complex version than does the early drama. The first encounter is that of Jack Burden, an idealist *manqué*, who has given up his work on a Ph.D. dissertation in history and gone into the harsh, practical world.[15] The ironies of Burden's slow but definite involvement with the complicated politician, Willie Stark, are formally designed to involve the reader with the narrator, perhaps more elaborately than he is with Nick Carraway of *The Great Gatsby* (1925). As Stark's successes make him more and more ambitious, the fallibilities of human nature involve him, Burden, and Burden's friends and relations, in a tangled web indeed. So the novel is not entirely concerned with Stark, though as an analysis of the homespun politician it is a superb achievement. At the beginning, he is a moral rookie, and he achieves a success as a result of both his own and his enemies' naïveté. The machine comes after the ideal, but the former is represented as being inevitable. No idealist survives the debacle of human and social involvement. Adam Stanton, one of the prelapsarian characters I have discussed above, suffers and dies from the very innocence he prizes most.[16]

The political machine which gathers around Stark turns out to be a composite of the public Stark; each part of the machine is a part of his nature. The good and the bad are unevenly mixed, and as he gets in more and more deeply and makes successive concessions to expediency, Stark plays dangerously with the mainsprings of collapse: first of his family cohesiveness, then of his political career, finally of his very life. In a sense, he moves ineluctably toward willing his own death (the web of circumstances involves the Stantons, Burden's "researching" into Judge Stanton's past, the disenchantment of Duffy, a political hack but a person capable of doing him much harm).

In the end, *All the King's Men* transcends its political context, and becomes a moral fable. More specifically, it might be subtitled *The Moral Education of Jack Burden*. Burden is truly, and drastically, a victim of circumstance; but he survives, and in that part of him that is left at the novel's end, he proceeds toward a knowledge and an awareness of history, and more explicitly, of himself. How he can do more than simply come to terms with that knowledge is a little hard to see after a heart-wringing and, in many respects, a dreadful experience. In expecting the reader to remain objectively free of involvement in, or even of empathic identification with, the life of Jack Burden, Warren is stretching his powers to their absolute limits. There are many paradoxes in the novel; the complexities of the Warren pattern are never so richly offered as here; it may be suggested that part of the difficulty comes from Warren's indulging in an almost unbearably rich texture. At times the literary circumstances seem to be victimized by him; at others, he seems to be led, with a fatal attraction, by his own richly endowed imagination. As in the patter of an improvising comedian, *some* things work and some do not, but all of them remain on the record.

Some ideas come through, or perhaps we should call them clusters of notions that haven't quite become hardened as ideas. One of these is Stark's assertion that good is "made out of badness" (*Men*, p. 272), Stark is trying to convince Adam Stanton of this; you just make up the good as you go along, he says (p. 273); and the run of "folks in general" (or society) simply bends and weaves to the moral necessities. In many respects, Warren believes this too, and Jack Burden is at least able to "take it in" after the calamities of the novel have run their course. Not so deep as a well, nor so wide as a church door: this is, roughly, the major metaphor of the limits of moral and political hurts. And Stark, who begins by suffering moral damage, ends both by giving and by taking it.

The counterpointing idea is that of the deficiencies of the idealist. Stark once more offers the text here: that "man is conceived in sin and born in corruption and he passeth from the stink of the didie to the stench of the shroud. There is always something." (*Men*, p. 203) Burden is forced (he yields to the man whom he started by supporting on idealistic grounds) to tap his way along a metaphoric wall, listening for a hollow sound. He finds several, the most agonizing of which makes him realize that he is the bastard son of Judge Irwin. But the Judge is not the only disillusioned idealist: Adam Stanton's body, riddled by bullets, testifies to the consequences of a stubborn idealism. Jack Burden's idealism, never quite accounted for by practical circumstances, is itself terribly vulnerable.

The society of persons in *All the King's Men* is a

mixture of men and women, each of whom has a *kind* of idealism; all of them are, in one way or another, victimized by the malignant tumor of expediency. In his having given these circumstances in all their rich and dense detail, Warren has produced a truly great book. But he denies us and himself much by relying upon Burden, who is too superficial, too easy to "ticket" and label, and is therefore a damaging influence upon the major conception of the novel. He is much more this kind of influence than was Carraway of *The Great Gatsby*; partly this is because of basic differences between the two novels: Fitzgerald's is organized cautiously, so that the images tend to sprout like Texas cabbages into symbols; Warren's book is *un jardin étouffant*. We are asked to attend to too much, more than we can safely comprehend. Yet *All the King's Men* is a most rewarding book. Seen in terms of the background I have all too sparingly given, its stature grows greatly and most gratifyingly.

ii

Of Caroline Gordon's works of fiction,[17] her second, *Aleck Maury, Sportsman* (1934), is the most illuminating; it tells us much about her primary concerns, as well as about the major symbols she employs to bring them to realization. Maury, who appears in or is mentioned in two other books, has a special interest because his acts and his eccentricities are somehow intimately related to Miss Gordon's special vision of the South and to her relation to a few of her contemporaries. Maury attends to the customs of his life with an almost fanatic persistence. Even though his interests seem scarcely related to the Civil War or to the decades following its conclusion, Miss Gordon eventually proves his importance. Maury's life as sportsman offers a fixed image of reality, a spatial image which incorporates all time and history. It is the image of a deep, blue pool, a "miracle pool," in an out-of-the-way place, fed timelessly by cool streams.

This search for the "still movement," the pure space is

by no means a sentimental act. Maury is, after all, much more knowledgeable about his world than Thoreau was of his; and he is far less lyrical and "literary" about it. Maury is at once a professor of Greek and Latin and a master sportsman. His sport is an occupation whose challenge has an infinite variety. Compared with it, the life of the scholar is diminished indeed.

Maury is a sportsman in the grand manner. The training of hounds, the impatient waiting for Novembers, the careful plotting of the course, finally the restraint of the hunt which postpones the kill—all of these convert the hunt into a very special kind of experience. The hunt gives Miss Gordon's novel a sense of time, as the deep, blue pool arranges its meaning in space. For Miss Gordon life needs to move in an orderly fashion from the fixed point of a patterned and naturally pure world toward a more stylized, a more formally ordered world. The progress from nature to tradition is never hurried, or at least we are made aware that it shouldn't be. One of the best clues to Miss Gordon's point of view is to be found in her occasional discussions of architecture: the cabins built in the slow moves westward of *Green Centuries* (1941) (as well as the clearings made for farming; the orderly cutting of trees in a pioneer setting is a form of "building"); the growth of the Brackets' plantation house in Virginia (*None Shall Look Back*, 1937) and of Penhally (*Penhally*, 1931); the contrast of the functionally appropriate Lewis farmhouse with Elsie Manigault's grotesque and alien manorhouse (*The Women on the Porch*, 1944).[18] Architecture describes family and tradition; the great achievement in cultural honesty in this kind of history is to civilize according to need and never beyond the limits set by need.

The *place* of Miss Gordon's fiction is simple enough; one sees it in an almost geographically pure line from Virginia to Kentucky and Tennessee. At the beginning of our history it is viewed as a succession of clearings, as men moved West. On the other hand, the people of her fiction are often a scarcely differentiated mass; they are held to lines of descent from the world's human beginnings, and they lack complexity. Many of her novels have this fault: *Green Centuries, Penhally*, and *None Shall Look Back* have a clutter of personalities instead of a wealth of characters.

The themes of Miss Gordon's fiction are as varied, and as conventional, as her concern with the region and with her family would lead us to expect. Some of them are the result of a sweeping look at the South's history: the Civil War's challenge to loyalties, its economic pressures upon families and estates, family divisions and declines, the postwar struggle to restore the land, the North's pressure upon the South. Others seem more closely associated with her own experience and family history: the stresses and strains of marriage with a scholar-intellectual, the conflict between the "Northern" (that is, the New York City) mind and the country temperament, the division of interests from one generation to the next. Finally, some of her interests are less profound than trivial; they come too simply, perhaps, from the "Agrarian" position assumed by her one-time husband and his contemporaries.[19]

The most satisfactory of all Miss Gordon's thematic concerns is the conflict between the sportsman and the intellectual. Extended, this relationship may also be seen in the differences between the Agrarian theorist and the urban sophisticate. Or, it may involve us in the contemplation of adult absurdities through the eyes and mind of a child (*The Strange Children*, 1951). As the root-source of all of these possibilities is the temperament of Aleck Maury and his knowledge of and respect for hunting and fishing. Maury is the true heir of the "whole man" of Southern history. The point of difference comes in the fates of the children: the boy, who might have been a close companion, is drowned in one of Maury's deep, blue, still pools; and the daughter turns away from the world he most likes, to another. He respects her choice, but there is always a feeling of uncertainty about what this division of interest means: in her case and his, who is the child, and who the adult? The question is never satisfactorily answered. For Maury's granddaughter, Lucy Lewis, who is quite naturally bored by adult chatter, it is obvious that the intellectual is a tedious fool (*The Strange Children*).

Miss Gordon's view of the adult intellectual has always been sharp; the intellectual is, after all, a person of limited experience. There is a brief glimpse, in *The Women on The Porch*, of Hart Crane, "a stubble-haired, pop-eyed fellow, who seemed to live only for poetry and had ended his life when it failed him . . ." [20] Something of this inadequacy haunts most of the intellectuals and artists of her fiction. The estranged husband of *The Women on the Porch* realizes this truth, as he travels to recover his wife. Words have interfered with past and present experience.

Miss Gordon's fiction comprises a remarkable range of literary discoveries. They are, in their own way, a fictional parallel of Ransom's poem, "Antique Harvesters." In stanza three, Ransom speaks of "one spot" of the land: it has "a special yield," quite different from the actual, the meagre harvest otherwise described in the poem. It is the yield of a tradition explored in fictional ways, and obstinately treasured beyond any evidence of a harvest on present ground. Miss Gordon has a sense of the South's total character; it is related intimately to Aleck Maury's vision of life and his realization that death will follow it. Her work has never been successful in the bestseller manner; its value lies in the emotional commitments and attitudes which stir it into being.

iii

Katherine Anne Porter has said many things about her career, her beginnings, her background; perhaps the statement most often quoted is this one, in a 1944 essay: "I am the grandchild of a lost War, and I have blood-knowledge of what life can be in a defeated country on the bare bones of privation." [21] This remark, among others, identifies her with the tradition of the post-Civil War South, and she is much concerned over the burden of the past, the proper perspective upon it, and the necessity to move from it into the present. This is only one part of her work, however. She is not in any way a regionalist or an historical novelist, but is instead preoccupied with the transformation of all life into art. She is a dedicated artist, and the experience of her and her family, back into several generations, comprises what she calls a "usable past," in the sense that memory, legend, personal experience, and required knowledge "combine in a constant process of re-creation." (*Days*, p. 123)

Nevertheless, much of Miss Porter's work is associated with the past; and one of the most exciting lines of development in her fiction is concerned with the special dispositions toward the past. Much of her fiction may be discussed under the title the "Miranda Story" because it is concerned in a very important way with a girl, Miranda, semi-autobiographical at the least, who must examine the past of her family, adjust to her disillusion with some of the memories and ritual clichés she has been asked to accept, and somehow settle into the image of herself as a person occupying space and moving through time. But Miranda is no ordinary, run-of-the-mill, *Gone With The Wind* heroine; partly her identity has been preserved from superficial attention because she has appeared in a number of places over a number of years, since her beginnings in the collection, *Flowering Judas and Other Stories* (1935).[22] The most important development of Miranda came, however, in the volume, *Pale Horse, Pale Rider* (1939).

Miss Porter's aim is not to reconstruct the past, in the manner of an historical novelist, but to show the disenchantment with the past and the burdens this experience puts upon the heroine. The imposing presence of the grandmother helps to maintain the legend; Miranda, of the third generation, has to suspend the legend so that she can examine it, and herself in relation to it.[23] In between the two, the transitional generation, there are a number of aunts, uncles, and cousins, who (along with parents) vary and confuse the issue of the legend and its acceptability. Miss Porter offers a portrait of the grandmother—this time, I must assume, directly autobiographical—in "Portrait: Old South":

[As she grew old] Her youthful confidence became matriarchal authority, a little way of knowing best about almost everything, of relying upon her own experience for sole guide, and I think now that she had earned her power fairly. . . . She believed it was her duty to be a stern methodical disciplinarian, and made a point of training us as she had been trained even to forbidding us to cross our knees, or to touch the back of our chair when we sat, or to speak until we were spoken to . . . (*Days*, p. 159)

In "The Old Order," [24] the grandmother is given us less sympathetically; she seems here to represent an order to which Miranda owes a loyalty she can only reluctantly give. The grandmother obviously goes back to the root-sources of Southern history, or at least of that part of it in the nineteenth century that antedates and postdates the Civil War. But experience settles into habit, and habit into dogma. From the position of both habit and dogma, the grandmother and her Negro companion, Nannie, judge the present:

They talked about religion, and the slack way the world was going nowadays, the decay of behavior, and about the younger children, whom these topics always brought at once to mind. On these subjects they were firm, critical, and unbewildered. They had received educations which furnished them an assured habit of mind about all the important appearances of life, and especially about the rearing of young. (*Tower*, p. 38)

The dramatic context of these remarks is in the first and the third parts of *Pale Horse, Pale Rider*. Since Miranda's mother had died, the grandmother assumed an extraordinary influence on her. Something was missing, and Miranda had to provide it herself; surely her move had to be away from the grandmother, and without the mother, she had to improvise the details of the change. Consider this pattern: it is so much superior to the ordinary "saga," because the full weight of psychological analysis is upon Miranda herself. In her first years, she was the ward of an old woman who sustained herself by the dogma of a legendary past. The insights of "Old Mortality" [25] are those of the third generation; Miranda must reject the formulas of the past, must fashion new ones for herself, and must somehow live with them. But there is a vast difference between the circumstances of generations one and three.[26] We discover Miranda and her sister (at that time aged twelve and eight years) at the beginning of "Old Mortality" with their grandmother, examining family memories and mementoes:

> Photographs, portraits by inept painters who meant earnestly to flatter, and the festival garments folded away in dried herbs and camphor were disappointing when the little girls tried to fit them to the living beings created in their minds by the breathing words of their elders. Grandmother, twice a year compelled in her blood by the change of seasons, would sit nearly all of one day beside old trunks and boxes in the lumber room, unfolding layers of garments and small keepsakes; she spread them out on sheets on the floor around her, crying over certain things, nearly always the same things, looking again at pictures in velvet cases, unwrapping locks of hair and dried flowers, crying gently and easily as if tears were the only pleasure she had left. (*Rider*, pp. 6–7).

The scene is an affecting one, and it demonstrates Miss Porter's consummate mastery over the art of setting up the right properties and proprieties. There is obviously a deep and wide abyss between the awkwardly drawn portraits and the dried flowers, over which the grandmother weeps, and the young girls, who, if they have an emotion at all, are merely embarrassed over the apparent necessity to have one. The clash of the romantic necessity and the push of the actual provides the first of Miranda's crises; she must first see these objects for what they are (though she can never really identify them, since their identity exists in her grandmother's memory); then she must reorganize her life in terms of the "actual," which replaces the rejected mementoes; finally, she has to walk bemusedly into the present time. The odor of past sanctity scarcely impresses her. And what happens in the family gives her even less assurance: the beauty of Aunt Amy proves to have been much exaggerated, as indeed has her virtue. There have been scandals, and these are imperfectly remembered and only reluctantly acknowledged. It is difficult to understand or to place the letter from great-great-aunt Sally Rhea: "In deep brown ink like dried blood, in a spidery hand adept at archaic symbols and abbreviations, [she] informed Amy that she was fairly convinced that this calamity was only the forerunner of a series shortly to be visited by the Almighty God upon a race already condemned through its own wickedness, a warning that man's time was short, and that they must all prepare for the end of the world." (*Rider*, p. 32)

Both the implicit character of these details and the extreme youth of Miranda suggest that the past is not going to be grasped, or appreciated, and it's certain that she is not going to, or cannot, use it for a model. Miranda's bemused curiosity over the past scarcely makes her equal to it; the details just don't make sense, and they shock and embarrass as much as they interest. In Part Two of "Old Mortality" the time moves forward two years; Miranda and her sister are in a convent school, in New Orleans. On invitation from their father, they meet the fabulous Uncle Gabriel for the first time; once again, the actual refutes the legend, displaces it in their minds: "He was a shabby fat man with bloodshot eyes, sad beaten eyes, and a big melancholy laugh, like a groan." (*Rider*, p. 46) What did grown-up people mean when they talked, anyway? Gabriel is now reduced to the sad limits of the lowest human denominator. Part Two offers one shock after another, dispelling any possible glamor the memory of keepsakes and cousins might still have had.

Miranda has grown up and has married in Part Three. The legend receives its final criticism; this time it comes from Cousin Eva, who was referred to earlier simply as "shy and chinless." (*Rider*, p. 11) Now, she has become a spinster teacher, a "very thin old lady" with "choleric black eyes" and "two immense front teeth and a receding chin" (though "she did not lack character"). (p. 62) Eva will, apparently, complete the job of smashing the legend that Miranda's initial doubts and her subsequent disillusions have already damaged. Amy, the fabulously beautiful Amy, was a "devil and a mischiefmaker" who "had enemies." (pp. 70–71) Eva's rather vicious exercises in puncturing the legend contain their own hints of weakness; she is obviously activated by something less than the purest motive; and Miranda does come finally to realize that what Eva is saying "is no more true than what I was told before, it's every bit as romantic." (p. 80) In the end we realize that Miranda has rejected both the legend and Eva's attack upon it. She must improvise her own views of the past; most of all, she must try to force the present. The family tradition has proved to her that she cannot rely for her own security upon the securities of others; worse, they have proved to be very weak securities indeed.

The Miranda story [27] has many additional ramifications. Many Porter fans prefer the title story of *Pale Horse, Pale Rider* to all of the others. Perhaps Nance's rather awkward division of Miss Porter's work into alpha and beta characters has a grain of truth in it; [28] it is certainly true that her stories seem to vary from those which suggest a milieu with which she conceivably might have been associated and those which treat of a world quite different from hers. But I should want to argue that she is much closer to the sensibilities of Maria Concepción and other "beta" characters than Nance is willing to admit. The great masterfulness of the second story in *Pale Horse, Pale Rider*, "Noon Wine," seems to me adequate testimony. In the *Yale Review* of Autumn, 1956, Miss Porter describes the experience of this story; from her own admissions the story obviously was vitally important to her, despite its not being concerned with the lives and loves of artists. "Noon Wine," she admits, is fiction; "but it is made up of thousands of things that did happen to living human beings in a certain part of the country, at a certain time of my life, things that are still remembered by others as single incidents; . . . So I feel that this story is 'true' in the way that a work of fiction should be true, created out of all the scattered particles of life I was able to absorb and combine and to shape into a living new being." [29]

The essay is a remarkable achievement in itself. What it tells us about "Noon Wine" simply reinforces our admiration of that story.[30] It begins with a deceptive casualness. There are no overt melodramatics. But of course "Noon Wine" contains much human tension and energy, which eventually explode into a series of calamities. The two men who face each other at the beginning, Olaf Helton and Earle Thompson, eventually are joined in the unconscious world of guilt and implication; but at the story's beginnings, Helton is merely a new hired man, with a few noticeable eccentricities. The two men begin in a series of differences: Thompson is "a noisy proud man," Helton a proud and quiet one, jealous of his privileges and eccentric beyond measure in some matters. Thompson's straight posture, signifying a pride of carriage and an immense self-esteem, is in one range of meaning like the stiff, mechanical, all but wordless movements of Helton's approach to him.

The minor strain of comedy involves these differences: Thompson's speech is hearty, broad, self-sustained; Helton's is terse, clipped, and intense. Neither man is capable of "seeing" the other; the only point of meeting is that of their complementary wishes: Thompson wants "women's work" to be done by someone beneath him (he wishes to prosper without exactly being morally responsible for his prosperity); Helton wishes to be left alone, to live his curiously narrow life as he wants to live it. Miss Porter's mastery of the story lies chiefly in her ability to move from what seem to be clichés about human conduct, into significant and even tragic finales. The relationship of the two Thompsons is another case in point; her objections to him at first appear to be quite trivial. But in the end she is forced to tolerate what is unbearable; her husband's eventual nature was there in the beginning and it is simply proved in its results. "She wanted to believe in her husband, and there were too many times when she couldn't. She wanted to believe that tomorrow, or at least the day after, life, such a battle at best, was going to be better." (*Rider*, p. 101)

As the time passes, Helton's obsessive diligence brings a change to the surface appearance at least of the Thompson farm. It becomes tidy, neat, in the manner of Helton's neatness and tidiness, and it prospers. The fact that prosperity returns to it is both a temporary good fortune and, ultimately, a disaster. For the stiffly mad gestures of the hired man must have come from a past that is liable to repeat itself. Helton is in one sense the tragic means of the story. Because he performs his tasks with a remarkable efficiency and scrupulousness, he preserves Thompson's dignity, recovers for him his prestige, and makes possible a nine-year period of peace and good fortune. But the deeper meaning of the story reveals itself only gradually. That meaning is suggested in several ways: for example, the matter of the harmonicas, over which Helton is ferociously concerned, surely indicates a madness; Thompson is lulled by the prosperity he enjoys into not really looking into Helton at all. Generally, Helton is treated by both Thompsons superficially; his madness is really made up, they think, of "crotchets" that are forgivable, and especially in the context of the "good" he is contributing to their lives. Mrs. Thompson's version of his madness is that he is "cranky": "The point was, to find out just how Mr. Helton's crankiness was different from any other man's, and then get used to it, and let him feel at home." (p. 104)

The story of "Noon Wine" suddenly erupts into violence and meaning. In as tense a passage as one may hope to find in modern fiction, the tone of the story changes radically. The new scene is quick, rich, and dense with new meaning. The heat of the August day becomes a living agent of the narration. The stranger, Homer T. Hatch, has come into the story to explain Helton to Thompson, a service which Thompson wants least of all. Hatch is a loathsome creature; there is no doubt of it from the start. But he is there in the role of devil's judge, and every gesture, every remark, serves as a kind of grotesque parody of Thompson's own nature. It is as though Thompson were glowering at himself in a mirror.

Now Helton's obsessions have been assimilated by Thompson. The noon wine song, which, Hatch explains is "a kind of drinking song," (p. 136) has a close relationship to Thompson; the "likker" in Thompson's case is his good luck, and that has depended on Helton. Thompson, in now "self-defensively" killing Hatch, is following through to the mad conclusion of "the drinking song." The murder emerges from the awful heat, as well as from Thompson's complex of irritations and fears. When he strikes Hatch, he sees things that do not exist, that are not happening. He kills Hatch crudely, bluntly ("as if he were stunning a beef") (p. 153), protectively, to save the self he had become in Helton's nine-year tenure on his farm. What follows is Thompson's inevitable fate. He searches for vindication, but no one (lawyer, judge, or fellow-citizen) can give it to him. He must therefore kill himself, still protecting his innocence at the very end, still insisting upon the circumstances he had believed he observed on that hot August afternoon.

To approach "Noon Wine" with predisposed attitudes toward what it should say is to do it gross injustice. Nance associates it with the "beta" characterizations—that is, he calls it a story which does not contain the semi-autobiographical "alpha" or Miranda protagonist.[31] Nance's classifications are achieved at some cost of simple good sense. Similarly, I find the critical reaction to Miss Porter's only novel, *Ship of Fools* (1962),[32] much too much handicapped by extraneous matters. *Ship of Fools*, says Glenway Wescott, "is a phenomenal, rich, and delectable book," and he proceeds to enumerate its remarkable properties: "the hallucinating specificity; the supreme and constant meaningfulness of everything; the bewitchment of the story as such, to be exact, the stories (plural) interwoven; and a continual sense of cause and effect, both in the mind and in external circumstances . . ."[33] I would want to add to Wescott's endorsement, that of Robert B. Heilman's analysis of Miss Porter's words, images, and scenes: she has "a very wide vocabulary," Heilman says, having already abundantly demonstrated the fact, "but no pet vocabulary; she has considerable skill in compositional patterns, but no agonized specializations of order." [34]

Despite these reassuring notes, I find that the prevailing criticism of *Ship of Fools* is much more like the review by Theodore Solotaroff, in *Commentary* magazine of October, 1962. He begins by denying the book any narrative virtues. "The main such weakness is that no effective principle of change operates on the action or on the main characters or on the ideas, and hence the book has virtually no power to sustain, complicate, and intensify either our intellectual interests or emotional attachments." [35] Mr. Solotaroff's objections come from a deeper source than these words would suggest. He complains that Miss Porter is consumed by scorn and hatred, that the "fools" therefore, and their surrogates in our own lives, contain no redeeming virtues. Partly, this objection can be traced to the imputed source of the title, Sebastian Brant's *Das Narrenschiff* (1494). The persons are *supposed* to be fools; their charm and idealism and virtue turn into idiocies. It may be that this leads to a monotony of characterization. It may also be that the model cuts off avenues of characterization and drama that should remain open. Wescott has a fine insight concerning the book:

> I told Katherine Anne this one day on the telephone, and she said, "I promised myself solemnly: in this book I will not load the dice. We all do it, even you have done it; and so have I in my day, as you well know. But this time, I resolved, everyone was to have his day. I would not take sides. I was on everyone's side."
>
> At that point I had reached only about page 100, and I replied to her, "Yes, my dear, but it might also be said that you are on no one's side." (*Truth*, p. 53)

Ship of Fools is a great book. On the surface, it describes a tedious journey, from Vera Cruz, Mexico, to Bremerhaven, Germany, similar to the one Miss Porter took in the early 1930's. That there is no mercy shown (an exaggeration surely) is an impression given by sensitive natures like Solotaroff, who want humanity to work easily within superficial categories. There is a form of *Weltan-schauung* nervousness in such reviews as *Commentary* that leads to an automatic rejection of books like this. Of course there are exaggerations—great ones, prodigious ones, but they turn out eventually to be quite appropriate. One petty malice (throwing the wretched dog overboard) leads to another, and to still another. Miss Porter's scenic narration makes her dependent upon lucky hits, on the way the images "come off." Superficially, the novel has an atmosphere of casual viciousness, but the light returns again and again, to the same assortment of fragile, stupid, even foolishly mad human beings. Why should she "insert" handsome, heroic persons, or turn the action suddenly into a happy line?

Ship of Fools is, of course, also a moral fable. As to the effectiveness of it as such, I am not prepared to say. Nevertheless, it is significant that one of the great symbologies of the 1930's to the 1950's (and beyond, of course, for Buchenwald and Hiroshima are agonizingly interrelated) is that of the Nazi moral blindness. We have already had some examples of it, but Miss Porter has given us the first full exploration of it. None of this has anything to do with the Agrarians or the South; it is all a product of a remarkable woman, an artist, a person of great wisdom, who has been able to go beyond tradition (as Miranda scarcely was able to go, or to little purpose), to face the present, to build upon the character of the present, and to offer a commentary upon it that is extraordinary rich and meaningful. It is a flawed book, of course (to say this is almost like saying that the begats of the Old Testament are rather tedious, don't you think). But it is also a remarkable achievement. Miss Porter's lifetime preoccupation with the short work, the scene, the suddenly revelatory object, and all of the virtues that are characteristic of the good short story and short novel, here serves her wondrously well. The novel is made up of flashes— moments, fragments, pinpointed actions or inactions (but that is what a ship's journey is, isn't it?). Yet they cohere; time passes, and the variety of characters somehow cover up for the fact that they rarely change, that their destinies at sea are implicit in their scowls and fears in Vera Cruz.

Ship of Fools is the product of an obstinate honesty. Miss Porter will take *no* sides. There is a deep, poignant compassion, nevertheless, in the vivid result. Above all, the inadequacies of the human being are given detailed attention. No broad, sweeping generalities are offered as indispensable to the narrative, or naturally to be inferred from it. Miss Porter reportedly spent some twenty years (with many digressions) in the writing. More important, her genuine skill, worked into patterns of fictional clarification, has culminated in a long book that continues to amaze and impress.

3   EUDORA WELTY
AND CARSON MCCULLERS

IN TERMS of career, Eudora Welty belongs to the middle generation of modern Southern writers. Her first publication was a short story of amazing effectiveness, "Death of a Traveling Salesman," which appeared in a Detroit little magazine, *Manuscript*, for June, 1936.[1] From 1936 through 1955 there was a burst of activity, with seven books, four novels, and three collections of stories published. Since 1955, with the exception of fiction and nonfiction pieces in magazines, she has slowed down considerably.

Since Miss Welty has spent much of her creative talent on places in Mississippi, the subject of place has been very important to her. Not that she is a regionalist, or a local-colorist, but that the qualities of setting are pre-eminently influential on her work. In an essay of 1956 she testifies to its role.[2] The novel from the start, she says

> has been bound up in the local, the "real," the present, the ordinary day-to-day of human experience. Where the imagination comes in is in directing the use of all this . . . Fiction is properly at work on the here and now, or the past made here and now; for in novels *we* have to be there. Fiction provides the ideal texture through which the feeling and meaning that permeate our own personal, present lives will best show through." (p. 58)

A few pages later she offers an arresting image, to facilitate our sense of place.[3] Some of her family grew up with a china night light, "the little lamp whose lighting showed its secret and with that spread enchantment."

> The outside is painted with a scene, which is one thing; then, when the lamp is lighted, through the porcelain sides a new picture comes out through the old, and they are all seen as one. . . . The lamp alight is the combination of internal and external, glowing at the imagination as one; and so is the good novel. Seeing that these inner and outer surfaces do lie so close together and so implicit in each other, the wonder is that human life so often separates them, or appears to, and it takes a good novel to put them back together. (p. 60)

The number of insights afforded here and elsewhere in her critical writing gives one a real sense of Miss Welty's sensitivity to her craft and of her conviction regarding its role as a means of "rescuing" and ordering life. The relation of appearance to actuality is indispensable: "Yet somehow, the world of appearance has got to *seem* actuality." Place (scenes, people in scenes, habits, *décor*, atmosphere) "being brought to life in the round before the reader's eye is the readiest and gentlest and most honest and natural way this can be brought about, I think; every instinct advises it." (p. 61) Elsewhere, she comes up with a definition of place in fiction as "the named, identified, concrete, exact and exacting, and therefore credible, gathering-spot of all that has been felt, is about to be experienced, in the novel's progress." (p. 62) [4] When it comes down to it, it is the explicit things that come through on the pages of a novel, that is, the physical texture. (p. 67)

These observations, brilliant as they are, set off a train of queries: *does* Miss Welty communicate "physical texture"? Doesn't she prefer the grotesquely fanciful to the actual? Diana Trilling, reviewing *The Wide Net, and Other Stories* (1943) compared the writing to the surrealistic art of Salvador Dali, with no intention of flattering either.[5] It is true that Miss Welty often chooses the fantastic elements of her scene, but they are no less real for having been thus chosen. Speaking about an old Southern community, she once said:

Indians, Mike Fink, the flatboatmen, Burr, and Blennerhassett, John James Audubon, the bandits of the Trace, planters and preachers—the horse fairs, the great fires—the battles of war, the arrivals of foreign ships, and the coming of floods: could not all these things still more with their stature enter into the mind here, and their beauty still work upon the heart? Perhaps it is the sense of place that gives us the belief that passionate things, in some essence, endure. Whatever is significant and whatever is tragic live as long as the place does, though they are unseen, and the new life will be built upon these things—regardless of commerce and the way of rivers and roads, and other vagaries." [6]

Her belief in the viability and continuity of place, of both objects and persons, gives her a philosophical sense of place. Certain places are known for being inhabited by "celebrities," who have left their marks upon them; the imagination, stirred by their extraordinary qualities, brings them back out of the past and reinstates them, thus repeating their lines, freshening them, and even in a sense bestowing immortality upon them. These observations apply to one of her novels, *The Robber Bridegroom* (1942), and to a few of her stories. But generally the places and people are quite commonplace. Griffith has described the geographical scope of them:

> For the most part, Miss Welty is content to confine herself to that special part of the South she has known so intimately in her own life: a section that includes not only the Jackson area, where her house has always been, but also the rich Yazoo Delta cotton country to the northwest and north (*Delta Wedding*), the red clay farms and hill country in the northeast and east ("A Piece of News" and "The Hitch-Hikers"), the pinelands and truck farms in the southeast ("The Whistle"), the New Orleans area to the south ("The Purple Hat," and "No Place for You, My Love"), and the Mississippi River bottoms to the west ("At the Landing"). [7]

In short, the range of place is fairly limited. The principal cities are Jackson, Natchez, and Vicksburg, Mississippi; there are others: in the volume called *The Bride of*

Innisfallen (1955), Miss Welty moves out into the "wide world" (Ireland, Naples, even into classical mythology, in "Circe"), not especially to her advantage. The stories are not necessarily improved for the fact of their expansion of setting. Similarly, one part of *The Golden Apples* (1949) is set in San Francisco, but the fact of San Francisco is the least of its virtues. She is best, I suspect I am saying, when she works with a setting and an atmosphere with which she is most intimately acquainted. Robert Daniel has pinpointed that area for us:

> by far the greater and the more distinguished part of [her fiction] has found its settings in the state of Mississippi. Sometimes it treats of the middle-class world of beauty-parlors and card-parties that presumably is Jackson; sometimes of villages in the Delta, with their storekeepers and salesmen and ill-to-do farmers, white and black; sometimes of decayed mansions in Natchez, and Vicksburg. And beyond all these, in her stories, lies the encompassing countryside of fields and woods and rivers, or even the primeval wilderness, when she writes of the region as it was a century and more ago.[8]

The actualities are there; Miss Welty has a clear idea of what she wants to do with them, of what she wants them to do for us. "Like a good many writers," she says in still another essay, "I am myself touched off by place. The place where I am and the place I know, and other places that familiarity with and love for my own make strange and lovely and enlightening to look into, are what set me to writing my stories." [9] Much more can be made of what amounts to both a critical theory and a theory of place and imagination, but perhaps the best way of testing what she says about her work is in the results of it. That work is only incidentally "grotesque"; it is grotesque only in the sense in which her subject is. She has an accommodating and a marvelously open imagination, so that both persons and things come through it endowed and charmed and identified as almost no other persons have ever been. To call these people weird, or unreal, or vague, is to testify to several misreadings of them.

It is true, as Robert Penn Warren says, that "almost all of the stories deal with people who, in one way or another, are cut off, alienated, isolated from the world." [10] It is also true that to concentrate upon this fact leads to a great distortion; and to say, with Diana Trilling, that her style has exceeded the legitimate uses to which it might be put,[11] is to go beyond the point of giving Miss Welty a chance. There are many eccentricities in her people, many oddities and vulgarities, which are given the fullest benefit of her style and talent. The peculiarities of character grow as a means of her style, which acts upon them in a manner that both clarifies the atmosphere about them and highlights those characteristics that need to be emphasized for full value. She is *committed* to her characters, and has promised them loving care, and sometimes sympathy, but no sentimentality. There is also much humor and much irony here, but they are not superimposed upon her people. Her people possess these qualities, or deserve to have them.

Perhaps the most obvious example is "Why I Live at the P.O.," a famous comic story from *A Curtain of Green*.[12] Here the narrator is neurotic as characters frequently are in Miss Welty's stories, but she sees to it that the character is taken at face value, and not for some museum specimen. The narrator explains why she has left home. Her sister, Stella-Rondo, was set against her; she'd run off with "This photographer with the popeyes she said she trusted." (*Curtain*, p. 90) A fierce competition results between the two sisters for the affection and approval of the family; we are, of course, permitted only the narrator's view of things, but that will serve. Stella-Rondo succeeds in setting the rest of the family against her; so, "at 6:30 A.M. the next morning," Uncle Rondo "threw a whole five-cent package of some unsold one-inch firecrackers from the store as hard as he could into my bedroom and they every one went off. Not one bad one in the string. Anybody else, there'd be one that wouldn't go off." (*Curtain*, p. 98) Right then, she decided "I'd go straight down to the P. O." (p. 99) So, here she is, at the P. O. in China

Grove. Of course there's not much mail, because "My family are naturally the main people in China Grove, and if they prefer to vanish from the face of the earth, for all the mail they get or the mail they write, why I'm not going to open my mouth." (*Curtain*, p. 104)

"Petrified Man" is another classic of folk humor and vulgarity. It is a collection of conversational gems gleaned from a group of women in a beauty parlor. The talk skirts around banalities and near-insults, and it finally settles upon the figure of the petrified man from the carnival, the "freak show." The three women chiefly involved in the discussion have long since gone past the point of loving their husbands, so the petrified man is an object of more than ordinary interest to the reader:

> "they got this man, this petrified man, that ever'thing ever since he was nine years old, when it goes through his digestion, see, somehow Mrs. Pike says it goes to his joints and has been turning to stone." (*Curtain*, pp. 40–41)

Subsequently, Mrs. Pike identifies the man as a man from the town, wanted for a number of rapes in California. She could have collected a $500 reward and finally is successful in getting it; but the "beautician," Leota, is furious to discover that she's used one of *her* magazines (she, Leota, should have had the reward, etc.) The humor and the horror are neatly blended; we are never really horrified by these people, yet they are ghastly and unpleasant and beyond hope.

By contrast, Clytie Farr of "Clytie" is almost entirely pathetic.[13] Clytie is from "The old big house," in the town of Farr's Gin, and she appears to be quickly losing her wits. The house is itself a ruin, in a state of semi-repose. As Clytie enters the hall, she finds that "it was very dark and bare."

> The only light was falling on the white sheet which covered the solitary piece of furniture, an organ. The red curtains over the parlor door, held back by ivory hands, were still as tree trunks in the airless house.

In ironic contrast is the diamond cornucopia which with her "wrinkled, unresting fingers" she holds; she always wears it "in the bosom of the long black dress." (*Curtain*, p. 157)

Clytie is obviously slowly dying (or going mad) from a lack of human love. She reacts sensitively to human faces, and looks at them searchingly, and with longing, hoping some day to find *the* face which will reconcile her to the world. But as for her family, it was not necessary to see *their* faces: their faces come between her face and another; "they prevented her search from being successful." It is the family that is killing her, driving her mad.

> It was their faces which had come pushing in between, long ago, to hide some face that had looked back at her. And now it was hard to remember the way it looked, or the time she had seen it first. (*Curtain*, p. 163)

She makes hesitant, tender, halting gestures toward human love. When Mr. Bobo, the barber who has come to shave her father, arrives, she reaches out to touch his face:

> . . . she put out her hand and with breath-taking gentleness touched the side of his face.
>
> For an instant afterward, she stood looking at him inquiringly, and he stood like a statue, like the statue of Hermes.
>
> Then both of them uttered a despairing cry. Mr. Bobo turned and fled, waving his razor around in a circle, down the stairs and out the front door; and Clytie, pale as a ghost, stumbled against the railing. (*Curtain*, pp. 169–70)

She is ultimately going to go the whole way toward madness. Her narcissism is of a special variety, the result not of love of self, but of fear of others. She sees her own face in the water of the rain barrel, "a wavering, inscrutable face."

> Clytie did the only thing she could think of to do. She bent her angular body further, and thrust her head into the barrel, under the water, through its glittering surface into the kind, featureless depth, and held it there.

When the old Negro servant finds her, "she had fallen forward into the barrel, with her poor ladylike black-stockinged legs up-ended and hung apart like a pair of tongs." (*Curtain*, p. 171)

These three stories are a fair demonstration of what Miss Welty was able to do in this amazing first volume. Perhaps one final look should give us—in a limited way, yet impressively—the very first story she published. The atmosphere of "Death of a Traveling Salesman" [14] comes close to being that of a fantasy, a dream-vision at the moment of death. As Mark Schorer has said, it is doubtful that the described action—except for the death itself—has actually taken place.[15] The salesman, R. J. Bowman, just recovered (or perhaps not?) from influenza, loses his way and wanders off into a "cowpath" and into the unknown. He has known hundreds of hotel rooms, but is now suddenly translated into an entirely different world. The car itself sinks into "a tangle of immense grapevines as thick as his arm, which caught it and held it, rocked it like a grotesque child in a dark cradle, and then, as he watched, concerned somehow that he was not still inside it, released it gently to the ground." (*Curtain*, p. 234)

Where am I? he asks himself. Everything has suddenly become passing strange, and his personality seems also to have changed; he wants, somehow to accept, to rest, just to be. At the door of the only house in sight, he finds a woman who is obviously with child. Inside the house, the darkness "touched him like a professional hand, the doctor's." (*Curtain*, p. 237) Images of expectant life and expectant death combine here. Bowman is not sure which one is promised here, or if both are. "He felt he was in a mysterious, quiet, cool danger." (pp. 237–38) But he chooses to be elated, overjoyed by a sense of life, a condition so different from the one he'd suffered most of his own life. The puzzle seems finally to be solved: he is in the presence of a fruitful marriage. Then, after much elation over his discovery, he takes his bags and leaves the cabin. He must get back to where he was before. But his heart attacks him once again; it begins "to give off tremen-

them. The many members are remarkable individuals; or, they are made to seem so by acts of nourishing each other's *amour-propre*. Hence, the opening passage, in which the Fairchilds' world seems boxed in by clouds and heat, is indispensable to the persistent design. Miss Welty plays with a light irony upon this uniformity, this family cohesiveness, which the landscape endorses and even duplicates.

> All the Fairchilds in the Delta looked alike—Little Battle, now, pushing his bobbed hair behind his ears before he took up a fresh drumstick, looked exactly like Dabney the way she would think at the window. . . . Laura felt their quality, their being, in the degree that they were portentous to her. For Laura found them all portentous—all except Aunt Ellen, who had only married into the family . . . (*Wedding*, pp. 14–15)

There is a surface appearance, at least, of permanence on the outside (they "never seemed to change at all"), but inwardly each of them was changing "every moment . . . an iridescent life was busy within and under each alikeness." (*Wedding*, p. 15) The family unity and "alikeness" continues into the cemetery:

> Here sweet dusty honeysuckle—for the vines were pinkish-white with dust, like icing decorations on a cake, each leaf and tendril burdened—perfumed a gentler air, along with the smell of cut-flower stems that had been in glass jars since some Sunday, and the old-summer smell of the big cedars. (*Wedding*, p. 132)

That this is a false continuity is obvious from the artificiality of the scene; Miss Welty opts for life, for "a smell of man's sweat," as against tombstones and antiquity.

Miss Welty's great powers of communicating essences through particulars sustains her throughout. Laura approaches the store, which is "like the pantry at Shellmound":

> The air was a kind of radiant haze, which disappeared into a dim blue among hanging boots above—a fragrant store dust that looked like gold dust in the light from the screen door.

Cracker dust and flour dust and brown-sugar particles seemed to spangle the air the minute you stepped inside. . . . All was warm and fragrant here. The cats smelled like ginger when you rubbed their blond foreheads and clasped their fat yellow sides. Every counter smelled different, from the ladylike smell of the dry-goods counter with its fussy revolving ball of string, to the manlike smell of coffee where it was ground in the back. (*Wedding*, p. 137)

The novel, lacking so much in plot in the conventional sense, is alive with activity and observation. Miss Welty makes much of the opportunities she has to engage in reflections upon the relations of humans to each other, within and outside of family bounds. "In the Delta the land belonged to the women," she says in one place, "they only let the men have it, and sometimes they tried to take it back and give it to someone else." (*Wedding*, p. 145) In the same strain, she observes that "of course those women knew what to ask of their men. Adoration, first—but least. Then, small sacrifice by small sacrifice, the little pieces of the whole body!" (p. 146) Persons, things, air, atmosphere: Shellmound is a place teeming with life, what Ruth Vande Kieft calls "a burgeoning home." [19] Of course certain people stand out from the mass, some because of circumstances, others because of one or another kind of daring or heroism. If there is narrative action, it has to do with Robbie Reid, the outsider who has married into the clan, then breaks away from it, only to return to the Fairchilds, humiliated but still inwardly rebellious. The marriage almost takes a second place, but it too is important for what it does by way of drawing persons together in a common interest. But the inner and outer worlds [20]—the landscape and the "souls" of the participants—are united as in no other Southern novel. The dust, the sky, the weather, have their human correlatives in Miss Welty's description of persons.[21] The following passage, which involves Ellen and George Fairchild, both of them extraordinary people, is a good example of her mastery:

It seemed to Ellen at moments that George regarded them, and regarded things—just things, in the outside

world—with a passion which held him so still that it
resembled indifference. Perhaps it *was* indifference—as
though they, having given him this astonishing feeling,
might for a time float away and he not care. It was not love
or passion itself that stirred him, necessarily, she felt—for
instance, Dabney's marriage seemed not to have affected
him greatly, or Robbie's anguish. (*Wedding*, p. 186)

The Golden Apples is a different kind of book.[22] Its
setting is scarcely larger, but it is more varied; and there
are more, and more widely varied, people. The scene is the
town of Morgana, Mississippi. In fact, most critics refuse
to call *The Golden Apples* a novel, and it is a collection of
stories in a sense; but the stories are vitally interrelated. If
anything, Miss Welty's skill and compassion unite here
more successfully than anywhere else in her work. To say
that this is her best work is not a popular judgment, but I
should want to place *The Golden Apples* very high indeed.[23] There has been much to do about Miss Welty's
use of mythological figures, and it is true that she has
always been interested in classical overtures; but the life in
Morgana can stand by itself, without the assistance of
parallels.[24]

Miss Vande Kieft has cited Yeats's poem, "The Song of
the Wandering Aengus," as the primary source; its last
line contains Miss Welty's title:

> And pluck till time and times are done
> The silver apples of the moon,
> The golden apples of the sun.[25]

To take these parallels too seriously (and Miss Vande
Kieft does not) is to put aside Miss Welty's genuine
concern for place and persons. King MacLain, who comes
close to being one of two or three leading characters, is
nevertheless treated shrewdly and with appropriate ironies. Generally, the disposition toward Morgana persons is
about what they deserve; they do not transcend themselves,
though occasionally they are victimized by ironic misfor-
tunes. Of the group, perhaps Miss Eckhart, spinster music
teacher, is the most accursed. Forced to care for an ailing
mother and deprived of romance by the drowning of her

one gentleman friend, she cannot answer to any ambitions or romantic impulses; so she relies upon the one pupil she has who shows a real talent, Virgie Rainey. She's the pride and joy, and the sustaining life. Miss Welty's description of the "June Recital" is most affecting as well as devastating: "The night of the recital was always clear and hot: everyone came. The prospective audience turned out in full oppression." (*Apples*, p. 62)

Eventually, Virgie goes into a movie palace to play the piano and loses all her talent and all her interest in serious music. A series of disasters finds Miss Eckhart in the county poor farm, from which point she essays revenge upon the house, upon the metronome (symbol and sign of her students' mediocrity), and upon her life generally. She sets fire to the old house, in the hope that it will be destroyed, but it is rescued by King MacLain and two other townspeople.

> Old man Moody and Mr. Bowles brought the old woman between them out on the porch of the vacant house. She was quiet now, with the scorched black cloth covering her head; she herself held it on with both hands (*Apples*, p. 76)

The Golden Apples turns to another young hero, Loch Morrison, who in "Moon Lake" (pp. 99–138) performs a rescue at a summer camp. The episode is masterfully told; Loch is obliged to plunge into a muddy and sticky lake bottom. All of his instincts turn him away from girls, whom he scorns, but here he must seriously attend to at least one of them. Two subsequent episodes concern the twin sons of King and Snowdie MacLain, Randall and Eugene. "Music from Spain" has its setting in San Francisco.[26] It is a strange story, of Eugene's admiration for a Spanish guitarist and of his encounter with him the day after his recital. He rescues the Spaniard from a near encounter with an automobile, and the two spend the day together, though neither speaks the other's language. Apparently Eugene returns to Morgana, and dies shortly thereafter. The last episode, "The Wanderers" (pp.

203–44), serves as a form of epilogue, summing up the lives of several Morgana people, commenting upon life in general. The key event is, appropriately, a funeral, in which Virgie Rainey's mother is buried. In death, she is decked out in the black satin dress, "the dress in which diminished, pea-sized moth-balls had shone and rolled like crystals all Virgie's life, in waiting, taken out twice, and now spread out in full triangle. Her head was in the center of the bolster, the widow's place in which she herself laid it. Miss Snowdie had rouged her cheeks." (*Apples*, p. 213)

Mrs. Katie Rainey, suitably the person who looks on, and listens, as distinguished from the active King Mac-Lain and Loch Morrison,[27] dies and thus provides Morgana with the only interesting social affair she has been able to give it. The funeral is a lively affair, and is enjoyed by all. It is, in effect, a reunion of the clan, from King MacLain (old now, and a tribal leader) to the smallest. Persons came, as they will come, from distant places as from near. Virgie "walked and ran looking about her in a kind of glory, by the back way."

> Virgie never saw it differently, never doubted that all the opposites on earth were close together, love close to hate, living to dying; but of them all, hope and despair were the closest blood—unrecognizable one from the other sometimes, making moments double upon themselves, and in the doubling double again, amending but never taking back. (*Apples*, p. 234)

iii

Lula Carson Smith was born in Columbus, Georgia, in 1917. The *Lula* she got rid of as soon as she could; she traded the *Smith* for Reeves McCullers' surname in 1937. She was, as the title of one of her short stories had it, a "Wunderkind."[28] Active from the beginning, anxious to "make something of herself" as soon as possible, she distinguished herself as a pianist, then in 1935 went to New York, apparently to attend the Juilliard School. She changed from music to writing, attended two or three writing courses at Columbia University, and published one of her early stories, "Wunderkind," in Whit Burnett's magazine, *Story*.[29]

The first product of apparent genius was the novel, *The Heart Is a Lonely Hunter* (1940).[30] While it is different from the novel that succeeded it, *Reflections in a Golden Eye* (1941),[31] and quite different from her best work, *The Ballad of the Sad Café* (1951),[32] it may be said that all of her work develops a single theme, the loss of love and the attempt of the self to identify with other selves. As in Miss Welty's stories, there is much said about and suggested of human isolation. John B. Vickery has perhaps best described the common situation:

> Love, then, is not to be construed in the romantic or sexual sense alone. Rather it is the measure of the heart's desire, the goal of man's quest, and the image of the world he lives in. Appropriately, the main characters in Mrs. McCullers' novels have a three-fold role—the lover, the quester, and the dreamer. However dissimilar they are and however different the object of their love, there is an essential kinship between Mick Kelley, the adolescent; Blount, the radical; Berenice, the Negro housekeeper; and Penderton, the army major with homosexual proclivities. For each of them pursues a dream in a world that is impatient with dreams and dreamers. In their most extreme form the alternatives with which they are confronted are to compromise or surrender, as Mick does when she gives up her music in order to contribute to the support of her family, or to remain faithful to the dream by rejecting all other claims, as Blount does.[33]

Mrs. McCullers had first thought of calling *Heart*, *The Mute*. On the basis of her plan for a novel of this latter name, she received a fellowship of $1500 from Houghton, Mifflin.[34] There is no doubt that *Heart* portrayed the essential loneliness of individuals; the deaf-mute is the center of all attraction and he becomes what each of the others will make of him: Mick Kelley, who like F. Jasmine Addams of *The Member of the Wedding* wishes to establish a rapport with persons outside herself, with a "We" which will eliminate the troubles of the "I"; Doctor Copeland, the Negro doctor, who is bitter and hopeful by turns and is caustically critical of the white world he is forced to live in; Jake Blount, who in his desire for companionship is given to "Marxist" denunciatory speeches; and Biff Brannon, who owns the café in which the others appear when they try to communicate with one another.

Mrs. McCullers' selection of a cripple is a part of her practice (witness Cousin Lymon, the hunchback of *Ballad*); that he should in this case be a deaf-mute and therefore unable to communicate with the others is even more to the purpose. It is even more significant that Singer should concentrate his interest in another deaf-mute, Spiros Antonapoulos, and thus remove himself further than ever from the normal world.[35] There is much here of the Sherwood Anderson *Winesburg, Ohio* conception of the grotesque. The essential desire fo her characters is to identify and to "connect," and both of these tasks are extremely difficult. When Singer commits suicide, the others are more disturbed than usual, because they have never really known whether or not they have "related" to him.

Her second novel, *Reflections in a Golden Eye* begins in this way:

> An army post in peacetime is a dull place. Things happen, but then they happen over and over again. The general plan of a fort in itself adds to the monotony—the huge concrete barracks, the neat rows of officers' homes built one precisely like the other, the gym, the chapel, the golf course and the swimming pools—all is designed to a certain rigid pattern. (p. 1)

The deadly monotony is bound to produce violence, which it does. Some of Mrs. McCullers' insights suggest that she had learned from D. H. Lawrence, and especially from the short story, "The Prussian Officer" (1917). The "dullness" Mrs. McCullers speaks of can generate neurosis and cause clashes and conflicts of temperament. Consider the pattern of persons and events: Captain Penderton is cuckolded by his wife Leonora, who has an affair with Major Langdon; Anacleto, the Major's orderly, is devoted to his wife; Private Williams is subconsciously Captain Penderton's lover (he has homosexual feelings about him, but does not actually indulge them).

This complex of human and inhuman relationships leads to several acts of violence. There is much "Lawrentian" tension between Penderton and Williams; then, one day Williams watches Leonora's nude body and is encouraged to visit the house; to have an affair with the wife of a superior officer is a high ambition. The first time he enters the Penderton house, he is reported by Alison Langford, who is committed to an institution, where she dies shortly thereafter. The next time, Penderton sees him and kills him. The Captain's acts of brutality, first with Firebird, his favorite horse, then in killing Williams, are both ambivalently motivated. Each time he is angry with himself for having acted as he had. As Evans says of this ménage, "the Captain burns with an impossible love for the soldier, and the soldier nourishes an equally impossible longing for the Captain's wife. The only successful relationship is the one between Leonora and Major Langdon, and this is successful only in the physical sense—a mere mating of animals." [36] *Reflections* probably deserved its rather disapproving press though there are some signs of talent in the development of a rather tightly knit set of plot circumstances.

All of the characteristics of Mrs. McCullers' work were realized in strange and wondrous ways in *The Ballad of the Sad Café*. Apparently the models for Amelia Evans and Cousin Lymon were taken from her Brooklyn experience; she had lived in a co-operative brownstone in 1940, with a number of poets, editors, and stage designers. In one of the bars on Sand Street, she noticed a prostitute called variously "Submarine Mary" and "The Queen of Heaven," one of whose favorite friends was a little hunchback. When the occasion demanded, she transferred both of them South to the Sad Café. The fact that it is a café again, like Biff Brannon's New Yorker Café and the café of the short story "A Tree, a Rock, a Cloud," [37] is typical; the café is frequently a public confessional, where (as is often true of Sherwood Anderson's characters) persons reveal the frustrations and inadequacies of their lives, in the hope that some younger person will gain from their mistakes. The café in the *Ballad* is not such a confessional, however; it is a place where the worst agonies of being are acted out. Oliver Evans says that *Ballad* "contains in a bare sixty pages the philosophy of her early novels, together with a fully developed theory of the nature of love." [38]

The setting is a dreary Southern mill town, boring, dull, and lonely. Here Amelia Evans is described at the beginning as living alone in a large house, all but one of the windows boarded up. Her face, as she peers out of the only unboarded window, is "like the terrible dim faces known in dreams—sexless and white, with two gray crossed eyes which are turned inward so sharply that they seem to be exchanging with each other one long and secret gaze of grief." (*Ballad*, p. 3) But the story is concerned with the past, with an explanation of why Amelia Evans had eventually come to that window, in that big house. Key to the change in her life is Cousin Lymon, the dwarf hunchback.

> He was scarcely more than four feet tall and he wore a ragged, dusty coat that reached only to his knees. His crooked little legs seemed too thin to carry the weight of his great warped chest and the hump that sat on his shoulders. He had a very large head, with deep-set blue eyes and a sharp little mouth. His face was both soft and sassy—at the moment his pale skin was yellowed by dust and there were lavender shadows beneath his eyes. He carried a lopsided old suitcase which was tied with a rope. (*Ballad*, p. 6)

The hunchback's arrival changes Amelia's life drastically; she had previously married a Marvin Macy, then scorned him and driven him out of her house. But, under the cripple's influence, she changes all of her habits; the general store now becomes a café, to which people can come, to get acquainted, to do things together; all of the townspeople are entertained. She herself takes on the look of a pleasant and happy person; or, rather, her appearance, from being that of a person stricken by sheer boredom to being that of one influenced at one and the same time by "pain, perplexity, and uncertain joy." (*Ballad*, p. 21) But Macy returns from his stretch in the penitentiary, foreboding misfortune and an end to her love for Lymon:

> The first person in the town to see this newcomer was Cousin Lymon, who had heard the shifting of gears and come round to investigate. The hunchback stuck his head around the corner of the porch, but did not step out altogether into full view. He and the man stared at each other, and it was not the look of two strangers meeting for the first time and swiftly summing up each other. It was a peculiar stare they exchanged between them, like the look of two criminals who recognize each other. (*Ballad*, p. 43)

Lymon turns to him, but Macy denies him; Lymon follows him around abjectly, hopelessly in love with him. Amelia, on her part, has not given up her love for Lymon. The three exist in this state of terrible (and comical) tension and friction. Knowing his power over her, he mocks her, imitates her walk, humiliates her; but she accepts him, will accept anything but his absence. Finally, in the climactic act, she throws herself upon Macy, furiously embittered over what he has twice done to her, but the fight is concluded when Lymon comes to his rescue.

> But at that instant, just as the fight was won, a cry sounded in the café that caused a shrill bright shiver to run down the spine. And what took place has been a mystery ever since. The whole town was there to testify what happened, but there were those who doubted their own eyesight. For the counter on which Lymon stood was at least twelve feet from the fighters in the center of the café. Yet at the instant Miss Amelia grasped the throat of Marvin Macy the hunchback sprang forward and sailed through the air as though he had grown hawk wings. He landed on the broad strong back of Miss Amelia and clutched at her neck with his clawed little fingers. (*Ballad*, p. 62)

This is the end of the "ballad." "Yes, the town is dreary." (p. 65) Miss Amelia, her hair grey, sits and waits for Cousin Lymon's return, and lives in utter loneliness.

The pathetic sequence of events sums up once more the theme of willed and wilful loneliness in Mrs. McCullers' work. Only this time the narrative is swifter, more sharply drawn and focused, and really quite superior to her earlier attempts to develop the theme.[39] As John Vickery says, the major feeling that is explored is that of lost communication: "the feeling of being trapped within one's own identity and unable to form a meaningful relationship with others leads to the idea of uniqueness and ultimately to freakishness."[40] *Ballad* is both the simplest and the most powerful expression of this feeling of entrapment. Vickery's explanation of the tortured relationships of the three "lovers" is quite satisfactorily clear:

> The archetypal pattern of love is presented in its clearest and simplest form in *The Ballad of the Sad Café*. For each of the three main characters is successively lover and beloved. Each, then, is in turn a slave and a tyrant, depending on whether he is loving or being loved. The refusal or inability of the characters to synchronize their changes of heart produces the interlocking romantic triangle which constitute the plot, while the grotesque comedy arises out of their each in turn conforming to a role they contemptuously rejected in another.[41]

In 1946, Mrs. McCullers returned to the world of childhood, with immense success. The world of F. Jasmine Addams, aged twelve, on the occasion of her brother's marriage, represents the problem of the trapped ego in a quite different setting—different even from that of the short story, "A Tree, a Rock, a Cloud." An awkward, impulsive tomboy with the power to spare, Frankie Addams tries desperately to "relate" to her brother, to his fiancée, to the Negro cook of the Addams household, Berenice. As Oliver Evans has said, Frankie is the "I" person who is trying to find a rapport with a "we" group—her brother and her prospective sister-in-law, in this case.[42] The distortions of behavior, however, are "cute"; in *Ballad* they were freakish and almost tragic. At the end of the novel, Frankie Addams has grown a year. She has relinquished the hope of joining her brother. She has suffered two losses: her little brother, John Henry, has died of spinal meningitis; and Berenice has left, to become remarried. But she is now "grown up" in the sense of being able to tolerate disappointment; and she has found another "we," a Mary Littlejohn. "She remembered John Henry more as he used to be, and it was seldom now that she felt his presence—solemn, hovering and ghost-gray. Only occasionally at twilight time or when the special hush would come into the room." (*Member*, p. 194)

The great popular success of *The Member of The Wedding* [43] established Mrs. McCullers as a novelist of some public reputation. She has since published one other novel, *Clock Without Hands*, [44] which is not a successful work. The plot involves a character, J. T. Malone, who has been told he will die in fifteen months at the most. There is much that is borrowed here, as well as much that is pretentious. Malone lies in the hospital, reading Kierkegaard's *Sickness Unto Death* (*Clock*, p. 147); he becomes very "philosophical," but endowing banal reflections with somber events does not give them dignity; or, at best, they bask in a reflected solemnity for only a short time. The "other plot" concerns Judge Fox Clane, a segregationist who is discovered to have a bastard son who is a Negro. The two situations and their interrelationships make for a disappointing sum—as though Mrs. McCullers had wanted to "go for broke" by mentioning everything she knew or had ever known. There is melodrama, involved as it is with the identity of Sherman Pew and his parentage. (See *Clock*, pp. 14–16) But the book does not hold up well, by comparison with *Ballad* and even the first two novels. [45]

There is, of course, every reason to believe that Mrs. McCullers may "come back." All indications are that both she and Eudora Welty have made substantial contributions to modern Southern fiction. Miss Welty is perhaps more subtle; she works harder, more consciously, with the form of her work. There are a number of cases when Mrs. McCullers has simply skimmed the surface of experience: surely *Clock Without Hands* and the play, *The Square*

Root of Wonderful, are examples of this habit. Nevertheless, these two along with Katherine Anne Porter and Flannery O'Connor, testify to a rather remarkable conjunction of feminine sensibilities in modern American literature.

4   JAMES AGEE AND FLANNERY O'CONNOR: THE RELIGIOUS CONSCIOUSNESS

IN THE Wesleyan College discussion of October, 1960, Louis Rubin raised the question of the South and religion, and was answered as follows:

> QUESTION: Miss O'Connor, you said yesterday that the South was Christ-haunted instead of Christ-centered. I don't quite understand this and how it affects our Southern literature.

> O'CONNOR: I shouldn't have said that, should I? Well, as I said, the South didn't seem to me as a writer to be Christ-centered. I don't think anyone would object to that at all. I think all you would have to do is to read the newspapers to agree with me, but I said that we seemed to me to be Christ-haunted and that ghosts cast strange shadows, very fierce shadows, particularly in our literature. It is hard to explain a flat statement like that. I would hate to talk off the top of my head on a subject like that. I think it is a subject that a book could be written about but it would take me ten or twelve years to do it.[1]

Miss O'Connor has written several essays on the subject, and it is obvious that her fiction is much concerned with it. There is the short story, "The Lame Shall Enter First," [2] in *Everything That Rises Must Converge*, a collection published posthumously. But I shall return to Miss O'Connor in the second half of this chapter. The religious consciousness surely varies as much in the South as elsewhere in the country; though it is predominantly evangelical Protestant, especially in the "Deep South"; and there is a passionate, deep, and violent feeling about the Bible and especially about the figure of Christ. Faulkner, who suggested the Christ figure often in his fiction,[3] did not go the entire way until *A Fable* (1954), and then described the Christ as a secular saint and model, following the Passion story generally but also careful to keep him on a non-transcendent level. In his talks at the University of Virginia, 1957–58, he was often asked about his use of the Christ symbol. One of his answers puts the matter rather clearly:

> Remember, the writer must write out of his background. He must write out of what he knows and the Christian legend is part of any Christian's background, especially the background of a country boy, a Southern country boy. My life was passed, my childhood, in a very small Mississippi town, and that was a part of my background. I grew up with that. I assimilated that, took that in without even knowing it. It's just there. It has nothing to do with how much of it I might believe or disbelieve—it's just there.[4]

James Agee's fiction is in several ways related to the problem. *A Death in the Family* [5] is an exploration of loss, the result of sudden death, which religious sentiment can scarcely alleviate. The novel was put together after Agee's death, so one is not sure that it is as he would have done it, or approved of it,[6] as it was published in 1957. Jay Follet, husband and father, dies suddenly in an automobile accident, and the impact is severe on his wife and on Rufus, the six-year-old son. In the opening passage (put there by the editor), Agee's descriptive powers are obvious enough. He is speaking of summer evenings in Knoxville in 1915 (when he was himself six years old): The "solidly lower middle class . . . middle-sized gracefully fretted wood houses built in the late nineties and early nineteen hundreds, with small front and side and more spacious back yards, and trees in the yards, and porches." (*Death*, p. 3) In one of these the Follets live, and Jay's survivors endure the shock of his loss.

The point of view is taken up mainly by Rufus' attempts to get used to the idea. Since he is only six, the impact is great but scarcely definable in its real sense. But Agee manages to work through him well. As for Mary, the widow, the experience is the first real challenge to her religious sense. As Aunt Hannah says to herself, "Her soul is beginning to come of age . . . and within those moments she herself became much older, much nearer her own death, and was content to be." (*Death*, p. 133) Agee is interested in a *moral* examination of human behavior, as Dwight Macdonald has said:

> By "moral," which has a terribly old-fashioned ring, I mean that Agee believed in and—what is rarer—was interested in good and evil. Lots of writers are fascinated by evil and write copiously about it, but they are bored by virtue; this not only limits their scope but presents a satisfactory account of evil, which can no more be comprehended apart from good than light can be comprehended apart from darkness.[7]

The great attractiveness of *Death* is that Agee explores the complex reaches of a human experience in a crisis, and, without overuse of its metaphors or doctrine, studies the powers of religion in relation to it. His analysis of the child's mind in this connection is especially acute. Here the mother is trying to inform Rufus and his sister of the death:

> "Daddy didn't come home. He isn't going to come home ever any more. He's—gone away to heaven and he isn't ever going home again. . . ."
> He stared at his mother. "Why not?" he asked.
> She looked at him with extraordinary closeness and despair, and said "Because God wanted him." They continued to stare at her severely and she went on: "Daddy was on his way home last night—and he was—he—got hurt and—so God let him go to sleep and took him straight away with Him to heaven." (*Death*, pp. 251–52)

It is Rufus who finally uses the word *dead*, startling his mother with it, because she has been trying so hard to communicate the fact without using the word. Rufus says the word over and over to himself. The mother finds the fact equally difficult to accept, and for a while her religious powers are paralyzed: "She had meant that she was sure that God would understand and forgive her inability to pray, but she found that she meant, too, that it really was all right, everything, the whole thing, really all right. Thy will be done." (p. 211) But the image of her husband continues to intrude, and she cannot yet banish it.

This is low-keyed writing, and it must be remembered that this is all there is. It is enough, for the complications of readjustment yield a long series of speculations and meditations whose complexity is all but inexhaustible. In the short novel that preceded *Death* by six years, *The Morning Watch*,[8] the intellectual and metaphoric sophistication is in one sense higher; that is, Richard [9] is in his adolescense and therefore his imagination is actively engaged with the religious issue. The figure of Jesus becomes a personal model, and for a while he becomes Jesus himself. Richard has been enrolled in an Episcopal school near his home in Nashville, Tennessee; he is now twelve years old. It is Holy Thursday, and Richard vows to stay up all night, hoping to come so close to the agonies of Christ that he will experience them himself.

As the day progresses, Richard marks off the events of the Passion as they had occurred so many centuries ago. Christ had been portrayed while Richard slept: "By now He stood peaceful before Pilate, the one calm and silence amid all that tumult of malice and scorn and guile and hatred and beating of unhabitual light through all the sleepless night of spring . . ." (*Watch*, p. 4) The truly critical day, of course, is Good Friday, and Richard is preparing his soul for that. Trying to comprehend the phenomena of Christ's sacrifice, of the Christian Grace, and of his involvement with them, he can only bring his mind back to the thought of death.[10] "Death: Dead, the word prevailed; and before him, still beyond all other stillness, he saw as freshly as six years before his father's prostrate head and, through the efforts to hide it, the mortal blue dent on the impatient chin." (*Watch*, p. 28)

Only now, Richard, after six years, is trying to conjecture the nature of his own death, as that is related to the death of Christ; if he can somehow suffer even slightly as much as Christ did, he will somehow come to terms with death itself. The mind of the twelve-year-old wanders; he is momentarily amused by the meanings of words; "Blood of Christ inebriate me" attracts him. How can Jesus' blood make me drunk, he asks. "Don't take it literally, he told himself firmly; but the literal words remained and were even more firm: make drunk. Intoxicate. Good ole whiskey, he suddenly heard in his mind . . ." (*Watch*, p. 33) A too literal acceptance of the metaphors upsets him:

> Within Thy Wounds hide me, he thought swiftly and with great uneasiness, hugging the ground and the leaf coverage as if beneath the skimming of a bird of prey: but try as he could, the image plunged and took him. (*Watch*, p. 34)

Then his mind drifts to sexual imagery. Shakespeare's *Venus and Adonis* and the words, "*he saw more wounds than one.*" (*Watch*, p. 34) Then there is a stay in his thoughts. It is the devil come to tempt him, he says (p. 35); and he prays to Jesus for the strength to resist.

The "simpering faces of Jesus" he had seen in pictures do not help. To enter into Jesus is becoming a task confused by many wandering notions and impulses. So he prays, this time fervently, to be rescued from the verbal and the sensual tangle to which he has invited himself. He turns to another series of thoughts concerned with his desire to become a saint. There are some suggestions here of the analysis Joyce gave to Stephen Dedalus in *A Portrait of The Artist as a Young Man.* Contemplating the prayer, "that with thy Saints I may praise thee," Richard rejects it as suggesting that it is a prayer for saints and near saints to say, and "nobody's got any business even hoping he can be a saint, he told himself."

> God no! he exclaimed to himself, for now suddenly it became vivid and shameful in his memory that he himself had for a while cherished, more secretly even than his lust, exactly this inordinate ambition. (*Watch*, p. 38)

But he *had*, actually, nourished such a wish; and he is in the act of once more entertaining it. *"Jesus, I my cross have taken,* he would sing, already anticipating the lonely solace of tears concealed in public: *all to leave and follow thee . . ."* (*Watch*, p. 40) "The whole crazy thing" had left him after Easter, but now it is returning: "he realized now with incredulous and amused self-scorn, he had ever more miserly cherished and elaborated his wretchedness in every one of its sorry ramifications, as indispensable to the secret, the solution, he had through God's Grace discovered . . ." (*Watch*, pp. 42–43) The forms of flagellation and self-mortification occur to him. The seriousness of the yearning is accompanied by flashes of the sense of its all being ridiculous. The thoughts culminate in his entertaining the prospect of his own crucifixion.

It was during one of these protracted and uncomfortable sojourns on his knees that his mind, uneasily strained between its own wanderings and efforts at disciplined meditation, had become absorbed in grateful and overwhelmed imagination of Christ Crucified, and had without warning brought to its surface the possibility of his own crucifixion. (*Watch*, p. 45)

The image of Richard nailed to the cross occurs to him, "a solemn and rewarding moment." But of course, in a deep country part of Middle Tennessee, it would be difficult actually to manage it. He could nail his own feet, but one hand would still hang free, "and it would look pretty foolish beside a real Crucifixion." (p. 46) He yields to the fantasy of Richard as Christ Crucified. His mother begs him to come down, but he rejects her pleas. A schoolmate turns to another, to whisper, "Jesus that kid's got guts." (p. 50) A photographer snaps a picture, and the newspaper reports "Strange Rites at Mountain School." (pp. 50–51) But whatever the community feels, God and Christ know and understand. But of course all of this has been an intense daydream, and "nobody seemed to have noticed anything out of the ordinary although he could not, of course, be sure of those who knelt behind him." (p. 52) Sanity returns, and vagrant images take him away from Christ Crucified. "Hell of a saint I'd make, he said to himself; and added with cold and level weary self-disgust to the tally of the sins he must soon confess, I swore in Lady Chapel in the presence of the Blessed Sacrament." (p. 61)

Good Friday having arrived, Richard reflects that "before this day is over he will be dead." (p. 85) It is *the* day in the symbolism of grace, but Richard thinks mainly of his self-involvement: "O Lord let me suffer with Thee this day, he prayed, his lungs about to burst." (p. 104) His act of self-mortification comes in the pond, into whose cold water he plunges, hoping to stay down "beyond the time, as an act of devotion." (p. 105) But he breaks the surface in time, "head back, gasping, feebly treading water, watching the streaming bruise-colored clamorous and silent whirling of the world and taking in air so deeply that his lungs felt as if they were tearing . . ." (p. 105). This surrogate crucifixion having been completed, he re-enters the world: "*Here I am!* his enchanted body sang. I could be dead right now, he reflected in sleepy awe. *Here I am!*" (p. 106) He has sloughed off his old skin and become renewed.

Then he encounters the snake, "a snake more splendid than Richard had ever seen before." (p. 107) He is the prince of another world; he is also a real menace in this one, "so that for a few seconds Richard saw perfected before him, royally dangerous and to be adored and to be feared, all that is alien in nature and in beauty: and stood becharmed." (p. 108) His two friends swash at the snake, but Richard turns them aside; he must finish the job himself: "he cared only for one thing, to put as quick an end as he could to all this terrible, ruined, futile writhing and unkillable defiance . . ." Finally, the snake lies "smashed and shifting among its debris," though the body, "even out beyond the earlier wound, lashed, lay resting, trembled, lashed." (p. 110)

In the adventure of the snake (the devil, whom he had not really stamped out of his life), he had forgotten what day this was, and the realization of his forgetfulness now comes back to him; he was, indeed, an indifferent saint, and surely not a Christ. The Christ imagery comes back to him, this time the Crown of Thorns. Here I am, he says to himself, as in the Passion Week the equivalent Christ is on his way up Calvary. God forgive me for forgetting, he whispers to himself. He determines to go without food this Good Friday: "The least I can do, he told himself. The *least* I can do!" (p. 118) The snake, it occurs to him, was still alive, and would always remain so, even though torn into pieces, and these pieces fed to the animals. The principle of evil is self-regenerating, and virtue is a painful discipline. With this, and with the boys' turning towards the main building of the school, the story comes to an end. The weight of guilt in his soul has diminished. Both it and the intensity of his Passion-Week dedication will, in short, be reconciled, for he must move normally through life—and toward his, and not Christ's, death.

ii

The best statement Flannery O'Connor has given of her purpose and method is in a talk at the College of Saint Teresa (Winona, Minnesota) in the fall of 1960. Responding to a criticism that she must not be a "Catholic novelist" because she doesn't write on "Catholic subjects," she said:

> The Catholic novelist in the South is forced to follow the spirit into strange places and to recognize it in many forms not totally congenial to him, but the fact that the South is the Bible Belt increases, not decreases, his sympathy for what he sees. His interest will in all likelihood go immediately to those aspects of Southern life where the religious feeling is most intense and where its outward forms are farthest from the Catholic. . . .[11]

Her major subjects are the struggle for redemption, the search for Jesus, and the meaning of "prophecy": All of these in an intensely evangelical Protestant South, where the need for Christ is expressed without shyness and where "prophecy" is intimately related to the ways in which men are daily challenged to define themselves.[12]

The literary problem raised by this peculiarity of "place" (though it may be located elsewhere as well, as a "need for ceremony," or a desperate desire to "ritualize" life) is neatly described as well by Miss O'Connor: she must, she says, define in unnaturally emphatic terms what would not otherwise be accepted, or what might be misunderstood. The sentiment (or some emotional reaction) will get in the way. "There is something in us," she said, in the same talk, "as story-tellers and as listeners to stories, that demands the redemptive act, that demands that what falls at least be offered the chance to be restored." [13] But the rituals of any church are not comprehended by a large enough majority of readers; therefore,

> When I write a novel in which the central action is a baptism, I know that for the larger percentage of my readers, baptism is a meaningless rite: therefore I have to embue this action with an awe and terror which will suggest its awful mystery." [14]

Miss O'Connor writes about intensely religious acts and dilemmas in a time when people are much divided on the question of what actually determines a "religious act." Definitions are not easy, and, frequently, what is being done with the utmost seriousness seems terribly naïve or simple-minded to the reader. She must, therefore, force the statement of it into a pattern of "grotesque" action which reminds one somewhat of Franz Kafka,[15] at least in its violation of normal expectations.

We have the phenomenon of a Catholic writer describing a Protestant, an evangelical, world, to a group of readers who need to be forced or shocked and/or amused into accepting the validity of religious states. The spirit of evil abounds, and the premonition of disaster is almost invariably confirmed. Partly, this is because the scene is itself grotesquely exaggerated (though eminently plausible at the same time); partly it is because Christian sensibilities have been not so much blunted as rendered bland and oversimple. The contrast of the fumbling grandmother and the Misfit, in Miss O'Connor's most famous story, "A

Good Man Is Hard to Find," is a case in point. The grandmother is fully aware of the expected terror, but she cannot react "violently" to it. She must therefore use commonplaces to meet a most uncommon situation:

> "If you would pray," the old lady said, "Jesus would help you."
>
> "That's right," the Misfit said.
>
> "Well, then, why don't you pray?" she asked trembling with delight suddenly.
>
> "I don't want no hep," he said. "I'm doing all right by myself." [16]

Another truth about Miss O'Connor's fiction is its preoccupation with the Christ figure, a use of Him that is scarcely equalled by her contemporaries. The Misfit offers an apparently strange but actually not an uncommon observation:

> "Jesus was the only One that ever raised the dead, . . . and He shouldn't have done it. He thown everything off balance. If He did what He said, then it's nothing for you to do but thow away everything and follow Him, and if He didn't then it's nothing for you to do but enjoy the few minutes you got left the best way you can—by killing somebody or burning down his house or doing some other meanness to him. No pleasure but meanness," he said and his voice became almost a snarl. (*Man*, p. 28)

One of Paul Tillich's most effective statements has to do with the relationship of man to Jesus Christ, in volume two of his most impressive *Systematic Theology*. "Jesus Christ," he says, "combines the individual name with the title, 'the Christ,' " and "Jesus as the Christ is both a historical fact and a subject of believing reception. . . ." [17] Perhaps more important, and in line with his attempt to review theology in existentialist terms, Tillich says: "Son of God" becomes the title of the one in whom the essential unity of God and man has appeared under the conditions of existence. "The essentially universal becomes existentially unique. . . ." (p. 110)

As all of us know, the crucifixion was historically a defeat for the messianic cause, whose followers wanted

Jesus literally to triumph over the Romans and to restore the Jews to power. But it was also, and most importantly, the source of grace; or, as Tillich puts it, " 'Christ' became an individual with supernatural powers who, through a voluntary sacrifice, made it possible for God to save those who believe in him. . . ." (p. 111) It is this latter figure whom Miss O'Connor's heroes spend so much energy and time denying; many of them also are on the way to accepting Him.

In almost all of Miss O'Connor's fiction, the central crisis involves a confrontation with Jesus, "the Christ." In the manner of Southern Protestantism, these encounters are quite colloquial and intimate. The "Jesus" on the lips of her characters is someone who hovers very near; with Him, her personalities frequently carry on a personal dia-logue. The belief, or the disbelief, in Him is almost immediate. He is "Jesus" made almost entirely human and often limited in theological function. Man often "takes over" from Him, or threatens to do so. The so-called "grotesques" of Flannery O'Connor's fiction are most frequently individual souls, imbued with religious sentiments of various kinds, functioning in the role of the surrogate Christ or challenging Him to prove Himself. Not only for literary strategy, but because such manifesta-tions *are* surreal, Miss O'Connor makes these acts weird demonstrations of human conduct: "irrational" in the sense of their taking issue with a rational view of events.

In terms of this interpretation the fiction becomes clear. Every conceivable change is rung upon the theme. The little boy, Bevel, in the story "The River," looks at a picture "of a man wearing a white sheet. He had long hair and a gold circle around his head and he was sawing on a board while some children stood watching him." (*Man*, p. 35) Later, he is convinced by the Reverend Bevel Sum-mers that the river is "the River of Life, made out of Jesus' Blood." (p. 40) And, finally, alone, he travels the route to his salvation:

He plunged under once and this time, the waiting current caught him like a long gentle hand and pulled him swiftly forward and down. For an instant he was overcome with surprise; then since he was moving quickly and knew that he was getting somewhere, all his fury and his fear left him. (*Man*, p. 52)

The association with water is simple enough. The rite of baptism is inevitably so associated; the extreme of the experience is drowning. In *The Violent Bear It Away* (1960) the young Tarwater, who is struggling against both his granduncle (who had demanded that he baptize the idiot child, Bishop) and his uncle (who tries to dissuade him), ultimately both baptizes and drowns the child, yielding momentarily to one demand, then in anger (or confusion) reacting violently to it.

The sensory vividness of religious imagery is especially stressed in the story, "A Temple of the Holy Ghost," in which the young girl has heard about a carnival freak, then later, in the convent chapel, faces God.

> Her mind began to get quiet and then empty but when the priest raised the monstrance with the Host shining ivory-colored in the center of it, she was thinking of the tent at the fair that had the freak in it. The freak was saying, "I don't dispute hit. This is the way He wanted me to be." (*Man*, p. 100).

For the child, as was the case in "The River," the evocation of Christ must be vivid indeed. The freak's acceptance of his freakishness is heightened by the quality of the last image of this story: "The sun was a huge red ball like an elevated Host drenched in blood and when it sank out of sight, it left a line in the sky like a red clay road hanging over the trees." (*Man*, p. 101) [18]

iii

The basic struggle is with "Adam's sin," or—to put it in less portentous terms—the natural tendency of man to sin, against his conscience, a disapproving society, or whatever metaphor he chooses to identify with his aberrant ways. The Christ figure is liberally used, and there is little true identification with theological explanations of Him. He is a weight, a burden, a task, even an enemy. Miss O'Connor's first novel-length portrayal of His effects is *Wise Blood* (1952). Here, Jesus is the object of attack when He is subject to exploitation along the lines of a "con man," collecting fees for salvation from easy victims.

The novel is charged with death and burial imagery. Hazel Motes, returned from the War to a town that no longer exists, goes on to the city of Taulkinham, there to start a new Church, "Without Christ." On the train, he lies in an upper berth, which reminds him of coffins in his past: "He was closed up in the thing except for a little space over the curtain." [19] He dreams, or half-dreams, of his grandfather, a circuit preacher, "a waspish old man who had ridden over three counties with Jesus hidden in his head like a stinger." Then he thinks of his father's burial: "He saw him humped over on his hands and knees in the coffin, being carried that way to the graveyard." (*Wise Blood*, p. 20)

Last things are with him as he moves toward Taulkinham, and "prophecy." Because his grandfather had always associated Jesus with sin, Motes decides that "the way to avoid Jesus was to avoid sin." (p. 22) Hazel Motes is one of a series of religious rebels whose rebellion and contrition are deeply personal. He must convince his fellow-men that there is no Jesus, or at least that Jesus is not necessary to the moral life, in accents similar to those in Nathanael West's *Miss Lonelyhearts*.[20] Motes fights the idea and the image of Christ; he also competes with a variety of other "prophets," including Asa Hawks, a fake blind man who insists that "you can't run away from Jesus. Jesus is a fact." (p. 51) For Motes, this is tantamount to saying that sin is a fact, and that he has sinned. He strives to solve the problem of moral conscience entirely without the aid of the Christ figure.

But he is so earnest, so frantic and stubborn about it, that it is obvious to anyone that he is obsessed by the challenge of Christ and will one day surrender to it. Meanwhile, he preaches "the church of truth without Jesus Christ Crucified."

"Every one of you people are clean and let me tell you why if you think it's because of Jesus Christ Crucified you're wrong. I don't say he wasn't crucified but I say it wasn't for you." (p. 55) [21]

The challenge is to begin a church which depends entirely on the defiant, soulless individual. Motes thinks that if he can control the theological circumstances, he will be able to set the terms of his morality. But things do not work that way. In a situation that resembles West's hero of *A Cool Million* (1934) and some of Samuel Beckett's, Hazel Motes deliberately, but slowly, destroys himself: first by blinding himself, then by exposing himself to the cold; finally he is discovered almost dead in a drainage ditch. "The outline of a skull was plain under his skin and the deep burned eye sockets seemed to lead into the dark tunnel where he had disappeared." (p. 231)

One of the more interesting facts of *Wise Blood* is its literally taking into account the necessity of redemption. In fact, in its own way, the novel describes in detail three stages of the journey to death: 1) the recognition of death (images of coffins and of long dark corridors and the "dark tunnel" of the above passage are corroborating evidence); 2) the rebellion against grace, against the idea of *depending* upon some figure or ikon, or supernatural being (this is, of course, as much as a rebellion against his grandfather as it is an act of violence against religion); and 3) self-immolation, or the individual move toward redemption. It is interesting that in the second stage, in "the big city" Motes goes "deep into" a "thin cardboard-smelling store that got darker as it got deeper," and emerges with a "glare-blue" suit. (p. 25) The color of the suit matches that of a cloudless sky, as if man's limits were nature's own. In stage three, the sheen of the suit wears off and it takes on a greyish, darkish appearance as Motes himself changes halfway into the cadaver he will appear finally to his landlady.

Wise Blood presents a powerful, mad resistance to the familiar pathways to redemption. The intensity of Motes's personal reaction is a deliberate underscoring of the religious story. Motes must eventually give way, and he does so, but not before he has had several very shocking and absurd experiences. He is proved to be unequal to the task of controlling his own fate; and his death is a parody of the death of Jesus. The landlady, looking into the sockets where once his eyes were, can see no eternity there, but a dark passageway through the skull. Meanwhile, in his efforts to establish a new church, he has attracted the attention of Enoch Emory, a guard at the zoo, an almost perfect "grotesque" representation of the "man un-known." Like Motes, Emory is trying to fulfill a mission, but he has a far more imperfect sense of what it is.[22]   Emory has a "secret," which he must show only to Motes. It is a shrunken (three-foot) mummified man in the city's museum. "He was naked and a dried yellow color and his eyes were drawn almost shut as if a giant block of steel were falling down on top of him." (p. 98)

This figure, which Emory steals one day and brings to Motes as a present, is Emory's idea of the "new Jesus." Since it has never occurred to him that Motes wants to do without Jesus altogether, Emory feels that he must after all be looking for still another version of Him. In a sense, Motes does believe in *a* Jesus, "one that can't waste his blood redeeming people with it, because he's all man and ain't got any God in him." (p. 121) But this kind of Jesus is beyond the power of his contemporaries to believe; Motes is, in any case, deeply engaged with his own inner struggles against his family and the fiery emphasis his grandfather had put upon grace and redemption.

In this semi-comic ooze of what one of the shyster preachers calls "Soulsease" (p. 156), only the absurd and the violent will have effect. Motes changes his course, from a defiant anti-preacher to a dedicated penitent, on the strength of a discovery that Asa Hawks had faked blindness, and did not have the courage to go through with the act of blinding himself, to prove that Jesus had redeemed him. Motes substitutes a real blinding, and becomes, abruptly, the young penitent, the self-appointed saint. To his landlady, "the blind man had the look of seeing something. His face had a peculiar pushing look, as if it were going forward after something it could just distinguish in the distance. . . ." (p. 214)

iv

This "something" is related to what the landlady calls "The eternal." It is also somehow akin to Motes's reversal (which is still as self-centered as the rebellion had originally been). He has gone the full route toward preaching the inutility of the Christ; now he will move back, to the point of self-inflicted immobility which enables him to join his relatives in the coffins he has remembered and dreamed about. There is so much of the extreme, the absurd, in *Wise Blood*, that it appears at least to be disjointed and all too simply plotted. Actually, every detail is part of a plan to portray the journey toward redemption in the setting of an extremely individualistic Protestant scene.

This journey is not only individualistic, but replete with suggestions of the Bible, particularly of the New Testament. Since Christ is a "prophet" in one sense, the Messianic sense, in which He is actively sought out as a savior in a moral *and* a military attack upon worldly forces, the opposition to him must be portrayed as a self-motivated "anti-Christ" attack, which is eventually atoned for by a personally maneuvered journey toward redemption. The action taken, the gestures, the decisions, are all non-biblical; and they appear absurd in the sense that none of them seems divinely inspired. In fact, they have the aspect of the diabolic. John Hawkes, in one of a few genuine tributes to Flannery O'Connor, speaks of her use of "the devil's voice":

I would propose that Nathanael West and Flannery O'Connor are very nearly alone today in their pure creation of "aesthetic authority," and would also propose, of course, that they are very nearly alone in their employment of the devil's voice as vehicle for their satire or for what we may call their true (or accurate) vision of our godless actuality.[23]

This is ingenious, and it is true at least insofar as it suggests the extreme remoteness Miss O'Connor's situations seem to have from anything verifiable in the Christian story. There *is* something "diabolic" in the scope of her heroes' opposition to orthodox Christianity; but eventually it can be seen as a struggle with the redeeming angels, so violent that it appears offered in a refracted light. For Miss O'Connor is for the most part describing two states of man: 1) the desperate need of redemption; and 2) the condition that exists in the absence (or the apparent absence) of redemption. These conditions have their own diabolic appearances, as in the Misfit's distorted version of the Pascalian "wager." [24]

We must eventually discover the meaning of her quotation from Saint Matthew, used as an epigraph of her most brilliant work, *The Violent Bear It Away*: "From the Days of John the Baptist until now, the Kingdom of Heaven suffereth violence, and the violent bear it away." [25] Violence is, virtually, a quality of the religious act in Miss O'Connor's fiction; it is also a signature of her characters' own personality, to testify to their approaching Jesus on their own initiative, after much and vigorous resistance, and their finally making a personal symbolic act in accepting him. In all of her fiction the way to salvation is dangerous, thorny, rocky, and devious; but there is this distinction, that her heroes put their own barriers in the way of achieving it.

In the situation of her last published book, the central figure, a young man, called just Tarwater after his granduncle, Mason Tarwater, is placed in conflict with two very strong influences: that of the granduncle's fiery demand that he baptize the idiot son of his uncle Rayber; and that of Rayber himself, the "rationalist," who believes that we are born only once and that we achieve only "ourselves." The violence exists within the three characters: the towering "two-hundred pound mountain" hovers over his nephew both in life and in death; the young Tarwater is anxious to remain free both of him and of Rayber; and Rayber, rather pathetically but also comically, opposes the old-time religion with the new rationalism.

As to the latter, it is obviously more an object of comedy than it is of serious representation. There is the matter of the hearing aid, made necessary because the elder Tarwater had once shot one of Rayber's ears full of buckshot. Tarwater the younger looks at the box outside him:

> He gazed briefly at the pained eyes behind his uncle's glasses, appearing to abandon a search for something that could not possibly be there. The glint in his eyes fell on the metal box half-sticking out of Rayber's shirt. "Do you think in the box," he asked, "or do you think in your head?" (*Violent*, p. 105)

The box does indeed at least affect his thinking, by intensifying his sense experiences whenever he turns it up. It distorts reality, despite (or because of) its being a marvel of engineering, the rational mind contributing an artificial aid to itself. It has bizarre effects, such as when Rayber is talking to the young Tarwater: he "heard his own heart, magnified by the hearing aid, suddenly begin to pound like the works of a gigantic machine in his chest." (p. 106)

Tarwater remains "free" of the persuasions of his uncle; he doesn't *need* his assertions of the rational "faith," nor does he intend to remember the irrational preachments of his granduncle. He "wore his isolation like a mantle, wrapped it around himself as if it were a garment signifying the elect." (p. 110) But he is not so free as he thinks. Memories of evangelical demands and warnings echo through his brain; and, while he remains coolly indifferent to his uncle ("I'm free," he says: "I'm outside your head. I ain't in it. I ain't in it and I ain't about to be.") (p. 111), in the end he too has an impact upon him. The impact is, ultimately, not rationalistic, but rather a communication of the quality and strength of conviction that have no respect for content. For Rayber is not himself wholly free of the contact with the irrational, despite his comical refutations of it. Ultimately, Tarwater's reactions to Rayber are violent (he baptizes the idiot child), and his feelings about both elders are stringent (he also drowns the child).[26]

Like Hazel Motes of *Wise Blood*, the young Tarwater must rebel against the act he is committed to sponsoring. Hence, he half agrees with his uncle, that "the great dignity of man . . . is his ability to say: I am born once and no more." (p. 172) But Rayber is also aware that Tarwater's eyes "were the eyes of the crazy student father, the personality was the old man's and somewhere between the two, Rayber's own image was struggling to survive and he was not able to reach it." (p. 115)

In these extremely unorthodox circumstances, the acts of the young man must be violent, must appear to be "diabolic," though they are at most the consequence of two basic drives: his desire to remain free of "the box" (the hearing aid, which he associates with Rayber's "enlightenment"), "outside" his head; and his resistance to the late granduncle's pressures. He is in a sense both doomed and free; for, though he says the baptismal words over the boy, he also drowns him: "The words just came out of themselves but it don't mean nothing. You can't be born again." This is a testimony to Rayber's influence, or to Tarwater's rebellion against the old man. "I only meant to drown him," the boy said. "You're only born once. They were just some words that run out of my mouth and spilled in the water." (p. 209)

There is something terribly confused in Tarwater's explanation. He is in the grip of these alien influences, yet he powerfully wishes to resist them. He is alternately under the eye of the old man and within the "box" (the mind) of Rayber. The acts committed are therefore both profane and solemnly virtuous. He is really trying to account for too much, and has somehow to act almost as if the three others (including the idiot boy, who is the victim) were acting for him. Miss O'Connor proves that the urge to religious action is present in all men: even in Rayber, who makes a fetish of proving his evangelically obsessed father mad; even in the idiot boy, who rides to his baptism on Tarwater's back.

In each case, the religious necessities take on a special image. They are madness to the old man's neighbors, "imprisonment in the irrational" for Rayber, "nonsense" to the truck driver who picks up Tarwater after the drowning. In the end, Tarwater is left with much to undo. He has sought to exorcise the spirit of his granduncle through fire (as he had tried to eliminate his body by burning the house). The fact is that none of his acts has been clearly a triumph: the drowning *was* a baptism after all; the house burning did not succeed in getting rid of the body. And, a murderer twice, once of his dead elder in an act of ritual monstrosity, another time of a small child, Tarwater must somehow return to the city, without true knowledge of the meaning of what he has done.

> His singed eyes, black in their deep sockets, seemed already to envision the fate that awaited him but he moved steadily on, his face set toward the dark city, where the children of God lay sleeping. (p. 243)

v

He has, in short, just begun to walk the path to redemption. But, while Tarwater stands out as a person of strong character, it is not his particular trouble that is important, except in the sense that it is exemplary. Tarwater has a much more confusing time of it than Agee's Richard. Miss O'Connor is dramatizing, in *The Violent Bear It Away*, the intrinsic necessity for grace in the human personality. The figure of Jesus haunts almost all of her characters. They are, half the time, violently opposed to Him (or, in His image, opposed to some elder who has tried to force His necessity upon them), because they cannot see beyond themselves to a transcendent existence. Hazel Motes and Tarwater are both haunted by the rank and stinking corporeality of their elders, whom they have seen dead and—in dream or in reality—have been obliged to bury.

These experiences serve to make them resist the compunctions of grace and turn away from the prospects of redemption. But the alternative is singularly uninviting. Hazel Motes has no success preaching the new church "without Christ," and Tarwater finds his uncle either pathetic or farcical. They react violently at the turn of their journey: Motes blinds himself in a mixture of the desire for penitence and the will to prove his courage; Tarwater has recourse both to water and fire, from mixed motives of defiance and fear.

This clarity of vision comes in part from Miss O'Connor's having had a satisfactory explanation of these religious drives, and therefore being in a position to portray the violent acts of those who possess the drive but are unable to define goals or direct energies toward them. The grotesqueries of her fiction are in effect a consequence of her seeing what she calls "the Manichaean spirit of the times," in which the religious metaphors retain their power but cannot be precisely delineated by persons driven by the necessities they see in them. Violence, in this setting, assumes a religious meaning; it is, in effect, the sparks caused by the clash of religious desire and disbelief.

> The novelist with Christian concerns will find in modern life distortions which are repugnant to him, and his problem will be to make these appear as distortions to an audience which is used to seeing them as natural; and may well be forced to take ever more violent means to get his vision across to his hostile audience . . .[27]

The matter becomes extremely delicate, in the light of her other observations: for example, that "art requires a delicate adjustment of the outer and inner worlds in such a way that, without changing their nature, they can be seen through each other." (p. 163) This remark suggests that the religious metaphors are, above all, psychological realities; that these are dramatized in the desperate struggles her characters have, at one time against but finally in the mood of accepting the Christian demands and rewards. When Miss O'Connor makes the following summary of her vision, therefore, she is simply defining the ultimate goals of her characters, whether they have been represented or not in the act of achieving them.

. . . I see from the standpoint of Christian orthodoxy. This means that for me the meaning of life is centered in our Redemption by Christ and that what I see in the world I see in its relation to that. I don't think that this is a position that can be taken halfway or one that is particularly easy in these times to make transparent in fiction. (p. 162)

5 THE MARK OF TIME: SOCIETY AND HISTORY IN SOUTHERN FICTION

A PEOPLE WHO have undergone a severe, even a traumatic experience, are bound to be interested in and puzzled by history; and the passing of time may make the images of the past more rather than less complex. The South was a special case of this kind of fate. In the 1930's many of the articulate spokesmen for the South believed that there was a virtue in the old order, and that it was being threatened from without. The argument is a bit simple-minded, as this illustration of it, from Andrew Lytle, will testify:

> Since 1865 an agrarian Union has been changed into an industrial empire bent on conquest of the earth's goods and ports to sell them in. This means warfare, a struggle over markets, leading, in the end, to actual military conflict between nations. But, in the meantime, the terrific effort to manufacture ammunition—that is, wealth—so that imperialism may prevail, has brought upon the social body a more deadly conflict, one which promises to deprive it, not of life, but of living; take the concept of liberty from the political consciousness; and turn the pursuit of happiness into a nervous running-around which is without the logic, even, of a dog chasing its tail.[1]

In his autobiography, *The Pavilion* (1951), Stark Young claims that his education at the University of Mississippi was not so much in "informed studies," but in personalities: "Partly by inheritance and partly by the way we live, our people came into an interest in human beings that was not so much psychological or analytical as it was

personal, secret, open, and bright with what is living . . ." [2]
Whatever the elements of truth in this, the fact is that
articulate Southerners, for a while at least, made a special
claim for the South, and for "tradition." They saw, and
defended, an image of society with a quite distinctive past.
This idea of a society stamped by time and yielding personal results, was presented for a while (in the 1920's and
1930's) as part of the war between science and society.
One of the peaks, or levels, of modern criticism occurred
when T. S. Eliot arrived at the University of Virginia to
deliver the Page-Barbour lectures for 1933. They were
subsequently published as *After Strange Gods: A Primer
of Modern Heresy*. His definition of a tradition matched
favorably and happily the efforts of his hosts to define
their past:

> Tradition is not solely, or even primarily, the mainte-
> nance of certain dogmatic beliefs; these beliefs have come
> to take their living form in the course of the formation of a
> tradition. What I mean by tradition involves all those
> habitual actions, habits and customs, from the most signifi-
> cant religious rite to our conventional way of greeting a
> stranger, which represent the blood kinship of "the same
> people living in the same place." [3]

This rather simple description of a traditional society
was echoed in many places by Southern critics. It is true,
as Stark Young said in 1930, "that we can never go
back." [4] And most critics recognized that the South was
changing, for good or for bad; and some of them doubted
that the image of what it was had ever really been actual-
ized, at any time. Nevertheless, the tradition *was* formulated, and as such it had an influence on modern Southern
literature. Briefly, and at the risk of oversimplification, I
should like to suggest that persons like Allen Tate, John
Crowe Ransom, Andrew Lytle, and Robert Penn Warren
thought a Southern tradition should be: first, a culture
that has persisted for several generations, in, secondly, a
fixed region, which has remained stable long enough for
the identification of customs, habits, and conventions;
third, life on the land, a co-ordination of moral and eco-

nomic responsibilities. With respect to the third, Allen Tate said in 1936 (also at the University of Virginia) that "in so far as [ante-bellum man] achieved a unity between his moral nature and his livelihood, [he] was a traditional man. . . . Traditional men are never quite making their living, and they never quite cease to make it. Or put otherwise: they are making their living all the time, and affirming their humanity all the time."[5]

There should also be a "native art," as distinguished from a "predatory" museum art.[6] And there is to be a code of manners, a ritual of customs, to put against a scientific or an "economic" or a simply "predatory" way of satisfying one's wishes. John Crowe Ransom, in one of two essays on Milton's *Lycidas*, arrives tangentially at a definition of this code.

> The aesthetic forms are a technique of restraint, not of efficiency. They do not butter our bread, and they delay the eating of it. They stand between the individual and his natural action and impose a check upon it. . . . To the concept of direct action the old society—the directed and hierarchical one—opposed the concept of aesthetic experience, as a true opposite, and checked the one in order to induce the other.[7]

ii

This image of a traditional society was not always operative; it served several polemical aims, but those who formulated it were aware of what a slender hold it had on the truth. The past of the South was a complex matter; the fiction which held a mirror to it varied widely. Perhaps the novel which most closely resembled the idea and the history of a traditional society was the only one published by Allen Tate, who otherwise used poetry and critical prose to advance his purposes. *The Fathers* (1938) is nevertheless a great achievement. It is a difficult, even a thorny book, but it forcefully presents the agrarian thesis, putting the traditional man against the "modern American." [8] The Buchans are of the old order,[9] and George Posey (efficient, a man of imagination) is the new man.

The novel, as John Stewart describes it, "is a superb example of what Tate himself later called symbolic naturalism, and what it symbolizes are the Agrarian ideas about cash-crop farming as a corollary of industrialism, the humanizing and restraining effects of a ceremonious society made up of families living in the country on their own land, the irresponsibility of capitalism, and Tate's own ideas about the trapped ego and the violence it does when not released by traditions and protected against the surging energies of sensation and impulse." [10]

Perhaps Tate could have developed beyond *The Fathers* and within its references, to become an eminent Southern novelist. He did not. The wonder is that, its "points" so surely made, *The Fathers* remains viable nevertheless as a work of literature. More or less in Tate's area of discourse (and a fellow "Agrarian"), Andrew Lytle has produced fiction that with a greater or lesser degree of directness sponsors the same position. In an essay which is chiefly a consideration of *The Velvet Horn* (1957), Lytle speaks of the fact and the history of a "Southern version of life that, discounting the sectional differences, had been common everywhere east of the Mississippi and east of the mountains." This life was destroyed by the Civil War, but the memory of it lingered. As a creative writer, he naturally and all but intuitively captured that memory. "To begin by wanting to resuscitate a dead society, it seems to follow, involves the writer in a great risk." He goes on to speak of the South as "a defeated society; and the defeated are self-conscious. They hold on to the traditional ways, since these ways not only tell them what they are but tell them with a fresh sense of themselves." What follows is an elaborate discussion of *The Velvet Horn,* and of the experience of creating it.[11] Lytle's work is directly involved with the tasks of creating the literary symbol, effecting a working compromise with "realism," and sustaining a myth from the conception of a culture and its past.

In a prefatory letter to Frank Owsley, in the novel, *The Long Night* (1936), Lytle speaks of the necessary purpose an agrarian society serves to literature: "neither man nor the arts can long flourish after the country loses its vigor, for this vigor sustains in one way or another all of the social practices, making it possible for the town to intensify, give form and expression to the common life." [12] *The Long Night* is itself a bloody tale of extended revenge; if my arithmetic is not inaccurate, the ratio of corpses eventually is eleven to one or two. The story is told by a Pleasant McIvor, who was the presiding avenger. His family, on the way to Texas, stops over on invitation from Tyson Lovell in Alabama, to test the way of life there. The father is killed, after having been falsely accused. Pleasant forces ahead, to account for those who assisted at the murder.

> In that part of the night when people sleep the hardest, our enemies slipped around the house as easy as smoke. Pa didn't hear them until they broke into his room. As he raised up in bed, Penter Wilton and his brother Jeems held him—ma saw them by the flash of the gun—while a man by the name of Fox shot his head off. (*Night*, pp. 53–54)

It is Pleasant's task to avenge the death of his father. That task takes him through two years before the Civil War, and through the war. It ends only when he sees the futility of it, and the fact that the human race is busy with more important things. He is endowed at the beginning with "a terrible patience and a terrible purpose." (p. 59) At the start he is assisted by kinfolk, but the main purpose is carried by himself. The "long night" serves his needs well.

> How easily he moved about them, while people slept in their beds, ignorant and helpless, trapped above or below, all of their strength wasted in the daylight. This was how his enemies lived—by the sun and open places, except for that one time when they had blundered about his father's cabin. (*Night*, p. 106)

One by one, the murderers are taken at night, by one stratagem of surprise or another. Then, the time arrives to do in Tyson Lovell, archenemy. Pleasant chooses the supper hour, when if ever the world is still and off guard. "I'm God's judgment, Tyson Lovell," he says to him. And Lovell answers him:

> "Come, come, my young savage. Let us behave like gentlemen. One may be brutal but never rude before the dark portal. I, who have sent so many through it, should know the amenities." (*Night*, p. 187)

But the announcement of the Civil War saves Lovell's life, for the time at least. In the army, Pleasant is always on the lookout for more victims. Another five are surprised and killed behind the Confederate lines. "He dragged them in different positions to make them look like they had been killed in a struggle, fired off some of their guns, emptied his own weapon, stamped the fire, wiped his shoes, and afterward ran to the rear, for in the distance he could hear the guard turning out." (*Night*, p. 202) But eventually "the old hatred" proves to have gone "a little stale" (p. 319); there were other loyalties, and in any case the will for vengeance had already supped mightily. The cause of the South now succeeded his dedication to his father's corpse.

> Twice he had loved—once the dead, once the living, and each by each was consumed and he was doomed. (p. 330)

The Velvet Horn is a much more subtle and complex achievement. Yet, in his explanatory essay, Lytle has explained his symbolic intentions clearly enough. "For example, in animal nature, the horn stands for both the masculine and feminine parts of being, the two aspects of the opposites which make a whole: the two in one contained by a single form. Add the velvet to this and you posit the state of innocence, that suspension before the act which continues the cycle of creation." [13] The novel is made difficult by hints and suggestions; unlike *The Long Night* it does not rely upon plot, but proceeds within the limits of a relatively few and static situations. Brewster Ghiselin's interpretation of it seems to me oversimple, but it does describe at least one of the author's intentions:

Lucius Cree, the young boy, "is enveloped in the life of the family, in an intimacy that bespeaks the fecundity and skill of Mr. Lytle's invention and gives evidence of his imaginative power." [14]

The Velvet Horn is, in part at least, the story of the growth toward manhood of Lucius Cree, whose apparent father, Captain Joe Cree, is killed by the felling of a great tree at the novel's beginning. In the end the tree is to be sawed up into lumber which will provide the enclosed space in which life may go on. Assisting him in this process is Jack Cropleigh, a man of all knowledges, shrewd in the ways of nature. Lytle depends much upon symbols, as we have seen; but he is also talented in the matter of the revealing particular, upon which he depends for more than just incidental effects.

> In the hatband [Lucius] smelled the sweet stale residue of himself and the dust from the mill had mingled with this odor, enriching it, reminding him first of the first real work, man's work, he had done. [15]

Growing up also involves Lucius' knowing about himself; but the knowledge (of his father who is not his father, etc.) must come slowly not only to Lucius but also to the reader. Lucius adjusts to the new information, because it has come when he is able to stand independently in terms of it. Ultimately, we are led to accept the lines of the family story, because the details are so vivid. *The Velvet Horn* is concerned with two Southern families in the Cumberlands after the Civil War. When Lucius finally comes to the knowledge of his parentage (that he is the bastard son of Pete Legrand, and not the son of Joe Cree), "It seemed strange to him that he had no feeling whatever about it. That was the strangest thing of all." (*Horn*, p. 371) The tree, which in the beginning had precipitated all of this searching and puzzling over his nature, is now to become the lumber for the building of a house. "He would watch every log cut and later, every board fall from the saw. And these boards he would take to raise a small house to bring his wife to." (*Horn*, p. 373) *iii*

William Humphrey has produced two novels that have essentially historical aims; they are histories of families, though political and military history also figures in them. Both of them are much crowded by effects; as the imagination deteriorates, the plots lengthen. Both have also been great popular successes. *Home from the Hill* (1958) is a story of the Hunnicutts in a small Texas town. It concerns the Captain's infidelities, the move toward maturity of the son Theron, the male world of hunting and sexual adventures. The young Theron is for a while an obsessive hunter, "with that bright image he carried always in his heart of his father resplendent in all his prowess and skill." [16] His growing up is measured apparently by his acquisition of skill in hunting. When it comes to a matter of love, his father's restrictions are unbearable; Theron wishes to have an unrestricted will in his affair. The girl, through his influence, "had made the great dreaded change, so quietly, so painlessly she had not known when, to womanhood." (*Hill*, p. 160) The plot becomes more and more complicated: Theron rejects his father, an irreparable change; Libby returns from the state university, carrying Theron's son; rejected by Theron, she marries a callow youth to protect her child's identity; and Theron leaves home. There is more of the same; convinced now that Libby's child is Wade Hunnicutt's, not Theron's, Halstead kills him. The novel ends in a hideously complicated involvement; Humphrey puts one complication after another. The best scenes are those of the hunt, especially those when Theron is a youth learning (as a poor man's Ike McCaslin) the intricacies of the forest and, presumably also, of God.

The Ordways (1965) is a romp through history and geography. While it has no more subtlety than *Home from the Hill*, there is some comedy, though even here many of the effects are derivative. The scene is Clarksville, in eastern Texas. "To get a start in life many of their children had had to leave home," Humphrey says, by way of underscoring its meagerness.[17] The formal device at the beginning is the town cemetery on Grave Working Day, when all the survivors of families are asked to freshen the graves of their ancestors. This frame gives Humphrey the opportunity to scan the past. "Before I could become myself," the narrator says, "as according to the biological law ontogeny recapitulates phylogeny, I would first have to live through the lives of those who had produced me." (*Ordways*, p. 20) There are many stories about Ordways (one of Inez Ordway's babies was eaten by a sow, for instance), but the two major stories have to do with journeys: the journey, at the end of the Civil War, to Clarksville; and the journey westward of his grandfather to recover a kidnapped son.

As for the first of these, the story of the narrator's great-grandfather, Thomas Ordway, "a specter haunting, a reminder of events which everyone wished to forget," it begins with the sight of his grandfather tending to the grave, and saying to himself, "Better if he had never been born." (p. 27) Thomas had been a soldier in the Civil War, and he had been wounded in it, so he was privileged to have a position of dignity at the Memorial Day services; but, in his stinking eminence he made everyone uncomfortable.[18] Then, the narrator describes the journey west from the mountain fastness of northeast Tennessee to Texas. As they learned that the South had lost, or was losing, the Civil War, the exodus increased. Thomas Ordway, blinded at Shiloh, revisited the site. He "found himself obliged to take pride in the courage, or that variety of fear called courage, which had blacked out his life past and to come and transformed him into a running sore." (p. 68)

By the hardest imaginable ways, the Thomas Ordways finally managed their trip to Clarksville—just managed, because almost everything not lost was squandered in crossing the river. The second journey is a picaresque chase across Texas, to recover a son. Humphrey cannot contain the events, so they become mock-heroic, provincial, and comical. The beginning—the father's guilt over the death, the childbirth of his wife, and his subsequent neglect of the child—is serious enough. Then, Will Vinson had stolen the child, and Sam Ordway's guilt whips him into pursuit. The chase lasts many days. In a long third section, called "Sam Ordway's Revenge" (pp. 149–323), Humphrey takes us on a Mark Twain ride through Texas. The seriousness of the occasion is seen only in Sam's persistence through all forms of accident and treachery. As in Faulkner,[19] Texas (or western Texas) becomes the great escape hatch, the place to disappear into if you want to get lost. The really serious and complex family matters are now lost from sight; they turn out not to be serious anyway. The novel becomes a comic-picaresque, not at all what it had begun being. From being an exploration in time (the cemetery, the War, the journey from Tennessee), it now becomes a romp through space, with what incidental interests and virtues it can pick up along the way. There are some evocations of the Texas landscape for which one might feel grateful. For example, "In such a landscape to come upon an anthill was a welcome diversion," and "There is no horizon. Rather, there is a horizon everywhere. The horizon is created whenever something or somebody stands up somewhere in the landscape." (p. 287)

The Ordways concludes with still another journey, this time for a reunion with Ned Ordway, uncle of the narrator, the boy who had gone west with Will Vinson. This time there is no mystery concerning destinations, and the trip is undertaken in automobiles. If it proves anything at all, this section demonstrates American mobility, the excitement of sheer motion; the matter of going hundreds of miles just for a visit, a commonplace event now, is here linked to a kind of pioneering, settling instinct. Ned Ordway, object of the search in Part Three, is now situated on a Texas ranch some seven hundred miles west of Clarksville; to it the family goes in fourteen cars. If Parts One through Three contain elements of dignity and concern, the atmosphere of Four is that of a trip planned by the Automobile Association. As David Hickey says, in a University of Texas literary magazine, *Riata, The Ordways* "is all narration and no drama and even though sam ordway (*sic*) has lost his son it is all travel and no quest and even if this is what mr. humphrey (*sic*) is trying to do that doesnt (*sic*) make it worth doing." [20]

iv

Shirley Anne Grau belongs to this chapter actually by virtue of one book; but since it is the most recent book and one about which there was some clamor, I have chosen to look at her work in this connection. Her earlier work strikes me as superior to the recent novel. The short stories, *The Black Prince and Other Stories* (1955), are quite good, some of them brilliant.[21] Many of them are about Negro life in the deep South, including the very fine title story which concerns the absolute pre-eminence of one Stanley Albert Thompson, a prodigy of strength and glory.

> It would have been simpler maybe if they could have fought Stanley Albert Thompson, but there wasn't any man keen to fight him. That was how they started fighting each other. A feud that nobody'd paid any mind to for eight or ten years started up again. (*Prince*, p. 54)

The story ends in mystery. Wilkie, who is jealous of the Black Prince, melts silver coins and shoots him with the bullets. That is the last anyone has seen of Stanley Albert Thompson, or of the woman he had charmed away from the others. Both become invested by gossip and folklore. "Miss Yellow Eyes" (pp. 72–115) is a New Orleans story of Negroes exploited and rebellious. Pete is angry about Negroes being so quickly drafted: "he looks more like a Negro when he loses his temper; it makes his skin darker somehow" (p. 82) Other stories (like "The Bright Day," pp. 145–63) are concerned less with issues, more with the precious quality of persons that Eudora Welty was so successful in evoking. "The Way of a Man" (pp. 181–212) is an ambitious story of violence: the young man lives with his old father, then is sent to the reform school, from which he emerges at the age of seventeen, "a man." A number of mishaps and discoveries lead to the murder of his father, and his maturity drains from him as he tries to escape capture.

> William looked down at the old man lying on the boards of the floor with the chair fallen over him and he shook his head. He had not meant to kill him. He lifted his arm and held it in the same position. He felt the muscles in his shoulder and along the arm. They had killed the old man. He had not done it. Not with his mind. (p. 207)

Some of the sharp, bright quality of the stories is carried over to the first of Miss Grau's novels, *The Hard Blue Sky* (1958); it would be hard to deny that this is her best work. The setting is a tiny island in the Mississippi-Gulf of Mexico Delta. The people in all of their poverty but also in their vivid presences are represented most successfully. Here life, while more sharply seen, is a bit like that of Steinbeck's *Tortilla Flat*, though the rigors of the weather make the life harder to bear. The novel culminates in a hurricane which devastates this highly exposed island. That is it: a faithful, a quite vivid record, true to the idiom of the scene and of its people.

The House on Coliseum Street (1961) is more ambitious and less successful. The house is an old one in New Orleans; it smells of much living in many decades.

> The house had a definite smell, she thought. And all the cleaning would never get it out. Because it wasn't a smell of dirt. It wasn't a smell of cooking. Or of anything in particular. It was the smell of the people and the things. Of the living that had gone on between the walls.[22]

But the novel is not about the 120 years, but about the present. The past is there, simply to cast a pall upon the present. That present is cluttered with human personalities: the mother five times married, with a daughter to show for each marriage; the children quite on their own; Coliseum Street, a shabby genteel residential area, living mostly in the memory of past wealth and privilege; the present husband living almost alone on the top floor, drinking seriously, surrounded by his Navy charts and books and "strange old-fashioned navigating instruments." (*Coliseum*, p. 56) While there is charm in all this clutter, one has only to read the title story of Katherine Anne Porter's *Pale Horse, Pale Rider*, to have a sense of how the scene and the idea might be best realized.

The Keepers of the House (1964) is by all odds Miss Grau's most ambitious novel.[23] The title is taken from Eccles. 12:3–5, source of at least two references in Eliot's *The Wasteland*.[24] The "keepers of the house" are successive women associated with successive Will Howlands. The book, for all its acclaim, is often badly written and haphazardly put together.[25] The novel opens with the figure of Abigail, who says "I feel the pressure of generations behind me," (p. 5) and "They are dead, all of them. I am caught and tangled around by their doings." (p. 6) What they were and what their doings were are the subject of the book that follows. It all started back in the early 1800's. Andrew Jackson's war (of 1812) was "a fine war, good and brisk." (p. 9) The first of the Will Howlands acquires the original property: William Marshall Howland, from Tennessee, who was murdered by Indians. The Howland boys took care of avenging the deed, and from then on the Howlands thrived. Every generation had a William Howland.

The new William "watched his house fill up with cousins and second cousins and great-uncles and -aunts by marriage." (p. 52) Then, after a long adventure and an exploratory journey into the swamp, Will meets Margaret, the earth-colored woman. He takes her into his house; he cannot espouse her because of her color, but he loves her and honors her and their children. "That was the way it began. . . . She lived with him all the rest of his life, the next thirty years." (p. 78) The "it" that begins is miscegenation, for which Abigail, a subsequent "keeper of the house," must suffer. Margaret's father, a surveyor of the new road, had been white: "She was black outside, but inside there was her father's blood." (p. 85) She bore Will five children, three of whom lived, two girls and a boy.

The final section is taken over by Abigail Howland Mason, the only white granddaughter; but she must take on the burden of the grandfather's miscegenation. The complexes of Negro and white blood in a set of family relatives are almost as complicated as the McCaslin genealogy.[26] The trouble happens when she marries a Tolliver, who becomes politically ambitious. He has to run on a segregationist ticket, of course, and his opponents are happy to find any information that might damage him. Before the crisis, however, there is prosperity; the house is redone by Tolliver, who recaptures its old style. "We were peaceful and smug and contented," Abigail says. (p. 230) "It's like this, when you live in a place you've always lived in, where your family has always lived. You get to see things not only in space but in time too." (p. 248)

News of the miscegenation is given out, and the gossip spreads. Tolliver leaves Abigail, alone, as keeper of the house. Indignant whites approach the estate, with the aim of destroying it. "That was all," she says in a brief epilogue. "The excitement and the fear left me when I saw that people had expanded whatever energy and violence they had within them." (p. 293) She tries revenge, with little success. In the end, "I went on crying until I slipped off the chair. And cried on the floor, huddled fetus-like against the cold unyielding boards." (p. 309)

v

There are many ways of reporting the moral consequences of miscegenation. Faulkner's fiction treats the subject brilliantly; even Sinclair Lewis handles the subject, in *Kingsblood Royal* (1947). Miss Grau's book is superior to Lewis'; yet, there is serious doubt in my mind if the treatment has to be so casual, so rambling, so repetitious. There are very good things in the book. Miss Grau has a genuine sense of landscape and weather and atmosphere, but she is not the master strategist of Southern history. Abigail's sobs at the end of the novel sound hollow to the ear. There is a real story there, a genuine and an agonizing problem, but she is many miles from

Faulkner's superb treatment of it. It may be that Walter Sullivan's *The Long, Long Love* (1959) is a kind of ironic commentary upon the "sore of the past." [27] The setting is Nashville, Tennessee, and an estate-village called Adam's Rest thirty miles south.

Sullivan's novel shines with opportune ironies. In Nashville, Horatio Adams (a marvelous combination of names) has a "fancy" big house, "three stories with turrets at the corners and as fancy as a river steamer with curlicues and stained glass transom." (*Love*, p. 11) Preoccupation with the past is a form of egoistic "wool-gathering." (p. 16) The "comedy" of the past begins with Horatio's regretting the fact that his parents have disappeared, without leaving a trace: "Their bones drifted somewhere in the ocean, washed by what water no man could tell." (p. 16) Adam's Rest, built by his great-grandfather in 1821, is his proper refuge. The life of Horatio Adams is superintended by disasters; his wife dies, a suicide. Why? She had left no note. He had never dreamed that "she would take herself from me." (p. 35)

What follows is complicated enough. Horatio remarries; Emily "was very beautiful," but there were also the Confederate monuments; (pp. 62, 72) his son acts strangely, and is seriously injured in an automobile accident. Then, worst of all, vandals have painted the Confederate statue "a bright, yellowish, nauseous green from the bottom of his boots to the very tip of his bayonet." (p. 88) The culminating disaster is discovered when the tombstone of General Adams is similarly desecrated. Horatio is deeply involved with death, cemeteries, bravery, and honor; he resembles, in his own Nashville way, Gail Hightower of Faulkner's *Light in August* (1932), except that the reader is not ever expected to take Horatio seriously. He decides that he will remove the General's remains from the public cemetery to the family estate; but, upon digging up the grave, he finds no remains at all. His daughter Anne reports the event:

> We stood with dour faces, and thought our dour thoughts, Emily pale and Father determined and Philip [Anne's

fiancé] trying to hide his morning joy and looking lugubrious. (p. 150)

The grim comedy continues. Horatio is caught reflecting that "I suppose when you have believed something all your life you cannot stop believing it, no matter how obvious it is you have been wrong, no matter how irrefutable the evidence." (p. 159)

The great Civil War general is not in the cemetery; then where *is* he? Horatio is serious enough about the whole thing:

> *It has something to do with all of us. What I want to find is something we can all be proud of, something that will stand with us against the steady course of time and the foregetfulness of man.* (p. 161)

Philip Holcomb agrees to investigate the wandering general's history; he is an assistant professor at Vanderbilt, so the task is not irrelevant to his interests. The search leads to Columbia, Tennessee, where General Adams had died, not in the heat of glorious combat, but shot by a jealous husband and buried back of the house. Two great Southern honors had conflicted: military and sexual; and, since the gun was conveniently near the offended husband, sexual honor prevailed.

The entire affair has its grim aspects; Horatio's son had run away with his wife and had been killed in a second accident. The son speaks up to his father:

> "All right," he said finally, "I'm a fool. But I'm a live fool and great-grandfather Adams is dead. And I don't mean to let a dead hero ruin a live fool's life." (p. 172)

What it comes down to is that the entire family has tolerated Horatio, who is an excellent chap, but beyond a certain point has refused to accept his fossil ideas. In the end, Horatio admits that he's been doing all his life what he'd done when he was a small boy: "trying to convince myself I wasn't Horatio Adams." (p. 230) Everyone has betrayed him, the General included; but the greatest betrayer was he himself.

Sullivan's book may be thought of as a masterful spoof. Surely the dull preoccupation with a past symbolized by an empty grave cannot be taken with the seriousness that was behind many of the essays in *I'll Take My Stand*. All of the elements of irony are there: the deaths (one by suicide, the other by a putative suicide) caused by a fool's obsession; the professor of history, using patience and the tools of his trade, discovering the trivialities that deflate an heroic legend; the accoutrements of tradition (Victorian gingerbread, monuments, and tombstones), which are a tawdry joke upon the living.

vi

Above all, the major burden of the Southerner has been the Negro. "Decent Southerners" are aware of the puzzling question which many Northerners have found hard to answer, concerning the equal intelligence of the Negroes. Some of the most important (and the most brilliant) Negro works have been the product, at least in part, of a Southern experience. Richard Wright was born in *Mississippi*; his autobiography, *Black Boy*,[28] describes the Negro life in the South. Ralph Ellison, born in Oklahoma, has produced some of the most effective of all analyses of the Negro's fight against the fact, as well as the farce, of white superiority.[29]

I am concerned here with the problem of the white's reaction to the Negro, his desperate attempt to accommodate himself to the freakish circumstance, the great majority push, irrational as it was and is, against the Negro's rights. Despite the impatience shown by James Baldwin, Stokely Carmichael, even Martin Luther King, it seems to me that Faulkner has presented the problem most deeply. Beyond and beneath the marching up and down, the attempts to duck around Governor Wallace or Ross Barnett, into the registrar's office, there is the *real* challenge of the Negro, Lucas Beauchamp facing up to Charles Mallison,[30] and all of the others in Yoknapatawpha County who provide telltale judgments of whites caught in moral mistakes or mere miscalculations.

There are many examples in Southern fiction. Almost no novel is without its Negro somewhere. But the main concern is with the problem itself. It becomes a political problem and it has always been a moral one. The political and the moral aspects of it conflict with each other; the tension is severe, leading to violence and death. One of the major dilemmas is that of the well-intentioned, liberal white (the "nigger lover," in the language of irresponsible whites) who tries to make political sense of his moral convictions. Elizabeth Spencer's *The Voice at the Back Door* (1956) comes bravely (though not very profoundly) to grips with the matter.[31] Part of the trouble with the novel is her desire to present a rather simple (though complicated) set of circumstances in a series of "delaying actions." To be brief: the sheriff dies of a heart attack; his widow gives Duncan Harper (football star and intellectual) an interim appointment. The upcoming election is troubled by a New Orleans based gangster group, who want to preserve the status quo ante and are willing to use mail-order rifles to emphasize their wish.

Duncan is one of the saddest creatures in modern Southern fiction. He *believes* in Negro equality, he has his standards; yet, he is badly mixed up, entertaining a mistress at odd hours and professing eternal fidelity otherwise. As we should expect, those public officers who are most approved are the ones who let well enough alone, who are all for the situation per se. I believe that Miss Spencer was right in complicating the plot as she did. Duncan's wife is loved by Jimmy Tallant; Duncan himself tries hard not to admit his love for Marcia Mae Hunt, who deserted him at a crucial moment (she was probably overwhelmed by his "sincerity" and couldn't stand it), but has returned after a failure in a quickie marriage. While these complications are "right," Miss Spencer's treatment of them is inadequate. The love affairs should never get in the way of politics; they do so because they are not presented as convincing love affairs.

Duncan's great "mistake" is not his opposing illicit liquor, but his sponsoring the Negro cause. It is here that

Miss Spencer is most successful. She has a real sense of the complexity of the Negro issue, though it may be said that everything she does serves a literary expedient. In 1919, twelve Negroes, who had approached the Judge on a matter of clear and decent justice, were slaughtered; the moral consequences live on into the present. In the end, the fears and doubts of the white population are complicated by the direct and vicious push of the New Orleans gangsters. Duncan is killed in an automobile accident, planned ahead and made inevitable; he had just before his death been deserted by his best, most "aristocratic" friends, who considered his liberalism on the Negro issue naïve, and certainly not politically expedient.

I have omitted many details from my report of this bloated tale. The author's ambition appears to have been to represent "everything." To take one example, Cissy Hunt, sought after by Kerney Woolbright—Yale graduate, lawyer, and crisply intellectual—was "that summer," poised "at a moment of femininity so intense that her virginity seemed scandalously out of order in the universe." (*Voice*, p. 159) *Plus ça change, plus c'est la même chose!* Miss Spencer should be congratulated for her great, intense, sincere intentions. But *The Voice at the Back Door*, a precisely articulated baritone at the beginning, declines to a gasp and a whisper before the novel ends.

IT IS A puzzling matter deciding whether a work of literature is prominent as a fantasy or not. What is a fantasy? For that matter, when can one call a novel a "Gothic" novel, or a detail (character, landscape, what have you) "grotesque"? Whitney Balliett calls Reynolds Price's *A Long and Happy Life* (1962) "so arty it is very nearly a parody of the Southern Gothic novel." [1] Stanley J. Rowland calls it this way: "Taut writing and acute observation are the major strength of this first novel . . ." [2] Apparently these diverse claims can be made about the same novel? This kind of contrasting reaction is not uncommon in the reviewing of literature.

What these terms—*Gothic, grostesque, fantasy*—have in common is some extension of the real, some elaboration upon the commonplace, the regular, the natural, whether for pure effect or out of inner necessity it is difficult to say. The term "Gothic" is used most frequently in contemporary reviewing when a novel is not "realistic"—that is, when it doesn't conform to normal expectations, when the author leads the reader down unknown, unfamiliar paths, or when objects are out of their natural order (the elephant in the swimming pool, the seal behind the bed, the talking portrait, etc.) All of this suggests contrivance. It may also be that the epithet used is a contrivance, an evasive device for avoiding the task of criticism. But beyond these expected reactions there is the world of the not-quite-real, the unexpected, in which human relations are described in something other than (higher than? weirder than?) situational terms. This atmospheric peculiarity is frequently employed to secure a more than ordinary impression or effect. The difference between saying "the August day was very hot" and describing it as follows is considerable: "[The land] seemed strummed, as though it were an instrument and something had touched it." [3] We have moved up one level, by means of a figure of the imagination. Just at what point our grasp of the situation *plus* the metaphor ceases and we have to speculate upon a variety of meaning is often difficult to say.

Eudora Welty has often been accused of straining credulity, and it is true that the setting of tone and scene in both of her first two volumes of short stories exceeds ordinary expectations. But, as she has several times said herself, this may simply be a matter of allowing the imagination to exact the maximum effect, through using as many effects as will effectively combine within the same particular and scene. Looking, for example, at one of the more effective stories from *The Wide Net*, we get this moment whose significance is immediately appreciated, though its precise meaning may take a bit longer to grasp:

> Fixed in its pure white profile it stood in the precipitous moment, a plumicorn on its head, its breeding dress extended in rays, eating steadily the little water creatures. There was a little space between each man and the others, where they stood overwhelmed. No one could say the three had ever met, or that this moment of intersection had ever come in their lives, or its promise fulfilled. But before them the white heron rested in the grasses with the evening all around it, lighter and more serene than the evening closed in its body, the circuit of its beauty closed, a bird seen and a bird still, its motion calm as if it were offered: Take my flight . . .[4]

There are four interactions. The three men relate to the heron, the heron to each of them, and perhaps beyond that the landscape and the precise moment (its exact atmosphere) relate to the reader. In any case, the detail has metaphysical properties far beyond those possessed by an ordinary scene visualized by an unimaginative person who has no power of exploiting what lies before him. As Miss Welty says, beyond the passage, "what each of them had wanted was simply *all*." Lorenzo Dow, the evangelist, wanted to save all souls; James Murrell, the bandit, wanted to destroy all men; James Audubon, the naturalist, wanted to record all natural life: "but now a single frail yearning seemed to go out of the three of them for one moment and to stretch toward this one snowy, shy bird in the marshes." (*Net*, p. 88)

Three men, each with a superlative wish, are halted in this still moment, in contemplation of a momentarily ideal scene in nature. They will go on, to murder, to save, to record, to create, as is their usual custom. But for this moment Miss Welty has got hold of them, and they must follow her will. Of course, this is not what her critics have in mind when they object to her violation of "the real." They are thinking of what they believe are direct, contrived particulars, beyond the call of necessity: like Clytie head-down in the rain barrel, discovered in the morning by the Negro woman, whose name is an improbable (so they say) Lethy; or the freak from the sideshow, in "Keela, the Outcast Indian Maiden"; [5] or the strongly transcendent experience of Mr. Head and his grandson as they see the Negro statue on the lawn of the white man's estate.

> Mr. Head looked like an ancient child and Nelson like a miniature old man. They stood gazing at the artificial Negro as if they were faced with some great mystery, some monument to another's victory that brought them together in their common defeat.[6]

Ihab Hassan notes the "gothic penchant" in the work of Carson McCullers: to say that she has it, he says, "is but to note, and to note superficially, her interest in the grotesque, the freakish, and the incongruous." He goes on, to suggest that these effects are related to a phenomenon he calls "alienation" (Oliver Evans calls it "isolation," which I suppose is a synonym), which is especially evident in the modern South. The "gothic," Hassan says, "insists on spiritualization, the spiritualization of matter itself, and it insists on *subjectivism*." [7] Of course, the example is *The Ballad of the Sad Café*, and there is no doubt that it contains phenomena that are extensions of the naturally "normal" reality. It is, of course, a question of what one is used to calling normal. Cousin Lymon, by his very appearance, is abnormal; his actions are similarly beyond or below the normal. The succession of events may therefore be called extraordinary; whether they are in consequence "gothic" would depend on an entire range of interrelated references.

One thing is expectedly true: in a society where intensities of behavior are frequent, the "gothic" is a kind of norm. Miss O'Connor's characters are often violently searching for a form of the divinity to relate to; they are themselves not always too articulate, so their rhetoric is often like the apparently aimless, though powerful, lashings by a snake of its tail. There are frightening and often puzzling details, which the reader finds difficult to fit into a context, so he concludes that they are "grotesque"; but "grotesque" is a word of many applications. A person may be "*a* grotesque," in the manner of Sherwood Anderson's *Winesburg, Ohio* characters [8]—that is, quite separated from normal behavior, gone mad in small ways; or he may *seem* "grotesque" to the reader, as are many of Welty's and O'Connor's characters; or he may in himself try to adjust to a "grotesque" world, thinking himself eminently normal in all he does.[9] As Hassan has said, these particulars of characterization are valuable only in so far as they help us to see characters in larger and larger dimensions. If they do not do that, they are speciously aberrant, unusual to no purpose.

ii

Truman Capote's *Other Voices, Other Rooms* [10] can perhaps best be described as a "romance" in Richard Chase's use of the term, which is to say Hawthorne's.[11] The young man, Joel Knox (aged thirteen), is taken from

New Orleans to a small Mississippi clearing called Skully's Landing. He goes there to see his father, and he is without a mother, facts that we need immediately to take into account. His arrival in Noon City, a few miles from the landing, is not auspicious; in any event, he is "too pretty, too delicate and fair-skinned; each of his features was shaped with a sensitive accuracy, and a girlish tenderness softened his eyes, which were brown and very large." (*Voices*, p. 4) The invitation from the Landing, which he had eagerly accepted, had the air of a call to an initiation; one needed to see one's father, in order to grow up.

At the plantation he meets Jesus Fever, an aging Negro, his face "like a black withered apple, and almost destroyed." (p. 29) Yet there was a touch of the wizard in his "yellow, spotted eyes," as though he could look into an extraordinary beyond, to which only he had access. The Landing is peopled by forms of provincial decadents. His stepmother Amy wore a dress "of an almost transparent grey material; on her left hand, for no clear reason, she wore a matching grey silk glove, and she kept the hand cupped daintily, as if it were crippled." (*Voices*, p. 41) She "fits into" the setting, a plantation house which is decaying, half of it burned down during the last Christmas holidays. There "was a lack of focus in her face" (p. 45), as there is a lack of focus in the surroundings. She is no less strange than Miss Rosa, of Faulkner's *Absalom, Absalom!*,[12] though she certainly has less narrative purpose and strength. Her real function is to be less attractive than Cousin Randolph, and therefore less a help to Joel in the forthcoming crisis. The crisis is foreseen in the embarrassment caused by Joel's insistent query about his father. It is obvious either that his father is absent altogether or that he has diminished in substance as a human being.

For the moment, he has to substitute a religious service for his father, a service conducted by Jesus Fever and his daughter, Zoo (Missouri). The substitution is not successful, for Joel is given to exact expectations and God is too remote really to answer him; and he cannot converse with someone so remote. Joel at this point, having left New

Orleans to escape isolation, finds himself more strangely isolated than ever before in his life. The sense of strangeness is increased when he sees his Cousin Randolph, a homosexual who will obviously try to win him over, away from his father and the emptiness caused by his dead mother.

> As he puckered his lips to blow a smoke ring, the pattern of his talcumed face was suddenly complete: it seemed composed now of nothing but circles: though not fat, it was round as a coin, smooth and hairless; two discs of rough pink colored his cheeks, and his nose had a broken look, as if once punched by a strong angry fist; curly, very blond, his fine hair fell in childish yellow ringlets across his forehead, and his wide-set, womanly eyes were like sky-blue marbles. (Voices, pp. 78–79)

This passage sets the terms of the conflict, in and for Joel's soul. Cousin Randolph has offered another voice, another room; its alternative, at the moment at least, is not a very attractive one (a dead mother, "friends" in New Orleans, attempts to take hold of "reality"—by which he means "normality" but does not presently know he means it). He tries to get away from the strange new circumstance, by staying in his own room, on a hot and dull morning, by writing letters to prove to himself that he does "connect" with persons outside of the Landing. The crisis becomes more serious when he finally sees his father, a shriveled up man, paralyzed and obviously close to dying:

> The eyes were a teary grey; they watched Joel with a kind of dumb glitter, and soon, as if to acknowledge him, they closed in a solemn double wink, and turned . . . so that he saw them only as part of a head, a shaved head lying with invalid looseness on unsanitary pillows. (Voices, p. 121)

Joel had seen death, or was near it, and he knew now that he had to escape from the Landing, because there was no father and the alternative was to accept Cousin Randolph as a substitute mother. Randolph begins to haunt him with the sheer perversion of his desires. He tells Joel of a past homosexual love: "with the garbage of loneliness stuffed down us until our guts burst bleeding green, we go screaming round the world, dying in our rented rooms, nightmare hotels, eternal homes of the transient heart." (*Voices*, p. 148) Randolph's appeal to Joel is not just a wilful and coy courting of his young manhood. He is at one and the same time trying to atone for an accidental shooting of Joel's father and to take the place of his mother in Joel's life.

With the death of Jesus Fever and Zoo's decision to move north, so she can see some snow before she dies, Joel realizes that he must escape now or never; this determination is all the more strong because Randolph has become more intimate with him. Tenderly, Joel takes his father's hand, as he informs him of his intention to leave: "it was, in a sense, the first time he'd acknowledged their blood; slowly he rose up and pressed his palms on either side of Mr. Sansom's face and brought their lips together: 'My only father,' he whispered, turning and descending the stairs, he said it again, but this time all to himself." (*Voices*, pp. 185–86) the leave-taking attended to, he is off to Noon City; but once atop a ferris-wheel in the carnival there, he sees Cousin Randolph's eyes staring at him from the darkness.

> Presently only a hatless man stood there in the emptiness below. Joel, his eyes searching so frenziedly for Idabel, did not at first altogether see him. But the carnival lights short-circuited with a crackling flare, and when this happened it was suddenly as though the man turned phosphorescent; he seemed to Joel no more than a hand's space away. "Randolph," he whispered, and the name gripped him at the root of his throat. It was a momentary vision, for the lights all fizzled out, and as the ferris-wheel descended to a last stop, he could not see Randolph anywhere. (*Voices*, p. 196)

A delusion, like the dream of his dead mother? We do not know, but Joel returns to the Landing, where he will apparently be under Randolph's control. The meaning of this strangely interesting book, surely Capote's best,[13] is perhaps best given by Marvin E. Mengeling, in a psychoanalytic examination.[14] The obvious facts are that Joel is approaching puberty, that he must make certain sexual and certain family decisions, that he is confronted with a dead mother and a diminished father, and that he must, finally, contend with Randolph, who, because of his sexual nature, is not a substitute father but will become as much a mother as Joel can know. His mother had died of pneumonia in New Orleans, in a cold, wet January, and Joel associates memories of her with snow and ice. Late one afternoon, Joel sees a "queer looking lady" in one of the windows of the house; it turns out to be Cousin Randolph.[15] Since he has been incapable of asserting his manhood with Idabel, the attraction to Randolph, for whatever psychological reason, is all the stronger.

When he returns to the Landing from his abortive attempt to escape it, he is desperately ill with pneumonia, the very disease that killed his mother. On his recovery, Joel recognizes the father image as "symbolically and psychologically slain." (Mengeling, p. 371) This is a convincing explanation of the path Joel has taken toward what appears to be a homosexual future with Randolph. It seems to me more precise than Ihab Hassan's explanation, which, stopping this side of psychoanalysis, yet driven by his desire for final meanings, ends by saying that "it is characteristic of Capote's nocturnal mode that the event should be presented in the guise of a trance or hallucination, a verbal *tour de force*, and that its moral force should be muffled by 'atmosphere.'" [16] It does not seem to me at all that the events of the novel are "muffled by 'atmosphere.'" Joel journeys into a real world. It is also a weird setting, but he reacts to it both visually and psychologically. There are "other voices" in "other rooms"; and, having resisted them for a while, he is forced by the circumstances of his having violated the memory of his mother to turn (in guilt and in a quite vague sense of expectation) to Randolph. Whether all of this is worth the effort or not is another question. But it does seem to me that for one time in his life Capote had almost successfully united his reports on outer and inner weathers.

If the world of *Voices* is a "nocturnal world," [17] that of *The Grass Harp* is a daytime world. It is still the world of a child, seen through the eyes of a child looking at child-like beings who act in obedience to a childlike logic. The years eleven to sixteen were "the lovely years" of the narrator's life. (*Harp*, p. 12) The tree house to which he and all like-thinking people go is "spacious, sturdy, a model of a tree-house, it was like a raft floating in a sea of leaves." (p. 17) The narrator, Collin Fenwick, is an upper-middle-class Southern Huckleberry Finn, whose interpretation of life is far weaker than his forebear's. To begin with, he goes with Dolly Augusta Talbo and Catherine Creek (the latter a Negro who pretends to be an Indian, by way of explaining the color of her skin), to gather bark for a remarkable medicinal recipe. When Morris Ritz arrives ("a hateful thing"), they plan to move out to the tree-house, and the conflict begins.

By accident, Riley Henderson, out shooting squirrels, comes upon the house. He spreads the news about it, and the townspeople are soon down upon them: Judge Charlie Cool, the Reverend and Mrs. Buster, Mrs. Mary Wheeler; and leading them, Sheriff Junius Candle, "who wore high-laced boots and had a pistol flapping on his hip." (*Harp*, 47) We very soon have the good guys lined up against the bad; the encounter is more formidable than one would normally expect it to be. From the beginning Judge Cool sides with them, and he initiates strategy talks as well as offers gems of philosophy: "spirits," he says are "accepters of life, they grant its differences—and consequently they are always in trouble." (*Harp*, p. 67)

The world, says Dolly Talbo after living in it for some time, is a bad place, so that the tree-house is a symbolic as well as an actual refuge from it. But of course it can only be a temporary one, because the world just won't let you live alone, away from it. After three skirmishes with the Sheriff and his party, the last one of which leads to some violence (Riley Henderson is plunked in the shoulder), the retreat is brought to a close. The Judge admits it's all been a dream; but "a man who doesn't dream is like a man who doesn't sweat: he stores up a lot of poison."

(*Harp*, p. 151) This is as profound as *The Grass Harp*
ever gets; it is of course, at a very low temperature, a story
of trapped innocence (or, the Rover Boys read Rousseau).
Paul Levine calls it a story "of a group of innocents, who
move into a tree house to escape the world and discover
their true selves." Since little of it can be taken very
seriously, it lacks the intensity of *Other Voices, Other
Rooms*; but it joins a rather large group of American
literary works, ranging in worth from Capote to Henry
James, which deal with the fact of innocence. It is notable
that the judge of reality in these works is almost invariably
a child, a teenager (Huck Finn, Maisie, Collin Fenwick,
et al.) who somehow "gets the message," and delivers it.
Such a European hero as Thomas Mann's Felix Krull [18]
learned about evil by participating in it; the prototypical
American hero discovers evil in the act of opposing it.[19]

iii

Far less well known, William Goyen [20] has an
achievement that is probably more substantial than Capote's. *The House of Breath* (1950) is a remarkable evocation from memory of the narrator's home in eastern
Texas; the voices speak out from it to remind him of their
and his past, as well as to identify themselves as persons.
This is a difficult point of view to achieve; the danger is
that all of the voices will sound alike, or that the net effect
will be that of a series of contrived echoes. Goyen avoids
both risks. "I came out and felt alone and lost to the
world with no home to go to," the narrator says, "yet on
the walls of my brain, frescoes." (*Breath*, p. 3) The name
of the town is significantly Charity; all living breath ema-
nates from it. The world outside is cold, and operated by
devious minds; it is a wonder that so many are so anxious to
get there. But, he says, "to find what we are, we must enter
back into the ideas and the dreams of worlds that bore
and dreamt us and there find, waiting within worn
mouths, the speech that is ours." (p. 10)

The narrator looks directly, in his imagination, at this
house of breath. In the hall there hung "a picture of a
blinded girl with a lyre, sitting on top of a blue, rolling

world and bent over in some sorrowful, lyrical telling-out of a memory." It was the song of the world's beginnings, of "the first man and woman naked and yawning in a garden." (p. 16) In the kitchen, on a map of the world, they had seen together "the brainshaped countries and livershaped countries where the whole mapped world looked like blooded lights of the dissected, opened out and pinned down body of the world as if it were an enormous fowl . . ." (*Breath*, pp. 18–19) Goyen's work most effectively outlines the particular scene (Charity's river) and its implications ("You were our Time flowing wrinkled and ceaseless over stones and roots," p. 22). Time, flow, sexual intercourse, life and death are all remembered in terms of the master image of the river: "You, River, then, held like a capsule of sperm the whole seed of creation; and the house we came from, breath breathed into it, like one uttered breath all the speech and all the life of man in a world of worlds." (p. 32)

The House of Breath is, in a sense, at the hub of the world. The narrator, like others, has left it to walk up and down in the land ("walking round in one's loneliness," p. 38); driven by ambition and restlessness, he goes off into the world much wider than Charity: "Yet when I looked in a showwindow I saw my terrible white face, lined and drawn like a dead man's." (*Breath*, p. 38) Goyen's novel is in this respect a study of place, seen from the perspective of out-of-place. He does have a theory of childhood purged and recreated in memory as pure humanity, "purged of that bile and gall of childhood." (p. 42) Going away, the narrator looks back upon the house, and repossesses it; the accent here is biblical: "The wheel is broken at the cistern, the rope at the well is raveled and rotten, the bucket is rusted and leaky." (p. 47) It is hard not to see the house so diminished in scope that it seems unreal, as the things of a child seem to him when he grows up and out of them. But also, the narrator is thinking here about the oncoming of age and death, "and the crops burning up under the burning sun and the teeth going bad." (p. 49)

The memory of the house in Charity is that of gut

hunger, and crops uncertain, voices echoing in the stillness, people no longer having anything to say to each
other, and finally the wind in empty rooms, the wind
"that winds a mummy cloth around the fallen splendid
house delivered to its inheritors." (*Breath*, p. 56) Then, a
picture of those in the family who went away: Sue Emma
(Swimma), for example, who went off to Dallas, to work
at J. C. Penney's, then, modelin', at Neiman-Marcus (p.
58); then onto the stage, where she made "a mint of
money I guess and became a real celebrity" (p. 60) Poor
Hattie Clagg, however, stayed at home and everyone depended on *her*; least aways, that is how *she* would put it:
"Benn a Christian all my life. Why, after all this, should I
be twisted with a twisted face and no one in the whole
wide world to call to me, 'Hattie, Hattie.'" (p. 75)

The basically simple philosophy informing Goyen's
book is of the intimate interrelationships of persons, who
are nevertheless locked, each one, in the prisons of themselves. The refrain is taken up by the narrator's mother,
whose complaint is somewhat different from the others.
Why, she says, there *must* be some meaning in all this; "it
caint all be rabblement and helter-skelter." (p. 100) The
narrator's brother was still another of the persons who
went away; his way led to death, but he took it anyway,
because he didn't want to sit in the small world of east
Texas; he wanted to *blaze* in the larger world. (p. 114)
Off with a circus, Folner wandered about, then felt the
great agony of loneliness and committed suicide in San
Antonio. It is hard, he had said, to be both "in the world
and bone of your bone." (p. 124) It is a miserable choice,
that between large ambition and elementary being.

The narrator has, after all, somehow to turn these reflections back into himself; and he does so by reciting the
marvel of his first hunt, "a terrible dialogue in the deepest
woods." (p. 159) Like Ike McCaslin's of Faulkner's "The
Bear," the hunting experience is both a lesson and an
invitation to wider and deeper experiences. The hunting is
a key to the narrator's life; it offers him the opportunity to
go far, to discover how we actually are, at best, a broken

lot. As he had gone out into the world, now he has returned to the house of breath, "built of the most fragile web of breath and I had blown it—and [it seemed] that with my breath I could blow it all away." (p. 181)

There are imperfections. At times Goyen has to come in with borrowed references, to the Old Testament, to Eliot, to Faulkner—or are these only the signs of "the first novel"? But *The House of Breath* is a remarkable performance. Once having adjusted to the technique and the point of view, the reader's understanding and interest grow mightily. The basic emotion of the novel is sympathy. Goyen is "living with" all of these people out of the past. Their driving wish—of both those who stay and those who go out into the vast world—is to find a meaning which will transcend the "helter-skelter," as the narrator's mother puts it. In other works Goyen tries to approach the same issue in other ways. *In a Farther Country* (1955) [21] seems to me modeled upon Saroyan and certain plays of Tennessee Williams and several others (I may simply mean it is *like* these works and doesn't really depend on them).

There is a frequent crisis of American fiction (it usually happens no sooner than the second novel) when a novelist is desperately concerned over means. This seems to me true of William Goyen. There is no doubt of his talent, of his keen sense of the lives of people, of his sense of engagement with them. It is a matter of just how to get this talent actually enveloped and contained. *In a Farther Country* is a badly flawed book. So much attention has been paid to the special mechanics of presentation that the meaning remains superficial too much of the time. The novel begins in New York City (it may also remain there, or it may never really have ventured east of some place in New Mexico), with Marietta McGee-Chavéz, a mixture of pure Spanish and pure Scotch-Irish. Apparently the spirit of romance is supposed to conflict with the blood of the Calvinists. A Spanish passion line "blazed a deep trail from the flange of her nose to the corner of her mouth, there lodged in this path what was plainly a mole and a family trait branded upon her by the Texas side, for all to see." (*Country*, p. 7)

Marietta is unhappy, lonely, and displaced. She compensates for her loneliness by visiting each day a large Woolworth's store; at first she takes pleasure in the plastics, then the birds in the pet department, and especially a "faded-out macaw" (or is it? Marietta insists it is a road runner who is also displaced and must return to New Mexico or die). (p. 22) It is "a strange combination of wildness and awkwardness, beauty and plainness, a frivolous, sad and wise creature adored by all and considered sacred and of good word and omen by the people of that country." (pp. 22–23) [22]

The atmosphere of Woolworth's is coy, charming, "interesting" (if one has the interests that go with arrested development). The setting is apparently shifted soon to the Southwest. Here, a succession of visitors, each with a deathlessly significant personality to offer, is introduced. Marietta lives in a house back of the shop "The Artifices of Spain"; and she is hostess of these remarkably strange and diverse creatures. Each of them airs out his "tragic soul, with a little gaiety." (p. 70) The situations that succeed one another are comic-grotesque; the meaning often tries to thrust forward and is pushed back. For example, there is Chalmers Egstrom, a large laughing man who carries with him a mandoline; the strings have been made from a switch of hair from the "head of my dead friend's sweetheart." They of course cannot be plucked, but "when I hang it on the wall at night over my bed it plays the most beautiful melody, over and over again, all night long." (*Country*, p. 90)

The persons who follow are, each in his own way, dedicated to the life of the "spirit" (that is, the beautiful simplicity of a pure world, with air like wine—vintage not specified). Oris, for example, born in England but for some time in Los Angeles, rises to recite a poem; but "only a long silence gathered round her shape that was like an annunication." (p. 99) There are others, each with his special charm and eccentricity; the plot, usually nonexistent, does occasionally manifest itself, like some persistent ectoplasm. Mostly, however, the novel is packaged with strange, quaint, and wholesomely informative lessons for the unenlightened.

"But there—we have forgotten what happens in the natural way of the world: the empowering, the increase that comes when the root waits and the sap suckles itself and enriches itself and the root has retired in the deep ground. In time we rise up again, self-nourished, into the fresh free world where the wildest and stillest and most passionate things may begin, again, to happen." (*Country*, p. 144)

There is much more; the episodes arrive accretively, spurred on by Marietta, the "Queen of Spain." The net effect is that of a lyrical sequence, dominated by a sense of what humans should be and qualified by the various overtones of human sounds of humming, laughter, poetry, and fable, until somehow we arrive at the last page, surprised to find outselves there, but grateful nevertheless. Goyen's great talent has somehow not been blessed by the quality of precision one sees in Katherine Anne Porter, Eudora Welty, and others of his compatriots. Yet there are flashes of brilliance. The story "The White Rooster" [23] is done with a fineness of comic perception and a precision that place it very high on an already distinguished list of short fiction in Southern literature. There is much here to suggest that Goyen could have been (might be, will be?) one of the first-rate Southern writers of fiction.

iv

Walker Percy's two novels [24] both depend much upon fantasy, decisions taken in odd circumstances, movements through and within widely disparate places. *The Moviegoer* (1961) is set in New Orleans; the narrator, Binx Bolling, manages a small branch office of his uncle's brokerage firm. The special quality of fantasy of the novel is the narrator's interest in motion pictures and their stars: "It is their peculiar reality which astounds me." (p. 21) He is considered a genius of some kind by his aunt,

though he admits that "actually I'm not very smart." (p.
50) Through college and beyond, high hopes have been
entertained of him; his aunt wants him to go to medical
school. Unable to cope with the actual world, he frequently settles for the cinematic one; there are degrees of
authenticity (for example, a movie like *Panic in the
Streets* with Richard Widmark was filmed in New Orleans and thus reaches a kind of ultimate in authenticity).
His behavior is modeled upon that of movie stars; toward
his society, "I keep a Gregory Peckish sort of distance."
(p. 66)

Bolling's worst problem is to "fit in"; the film world
seems to give a greater sense of security and correctness
than any other. Memories of films are more vivid than
those of past experiences. Bolling has a special fondness
for what he calls "a repetition," which he describes as "the
re-enactment of past experience toward the end of isolating the time segment which has lapsed in order that it, the
lapsed time, can be savored of itself and without the usual
adulterations of events that clog time like peanuts in
brittle." (p. 77) Thus a repetition is a "clean" recurrence,
free of extraneous mixtures and adhesions. For example,
the two seeings of *The Ox-Bow Incident* are fourteen
years apart, but they click perfectly: "There we sat, I in
the same seat I think, and afterwards came out into the
smell of privet. Camphor berries popped underfoot on the
same section of broken pavement." (pp. 76–77)

Bolling's real problem is to put together segments of his
experience. He suffers badly from insomnia, and hasn't
really lost consciousness since he was a child. He lives in a
condition of suspended consciousness and he tries to ma-
neuver the parts of himself into some reasonable, or at
least tolerable, pattern. He feels a sympathetic conjunction with Jews, for example: "We share the same exile,"
except that Jews are "more at home than I am. I accept
my exile." (p. 85) Searching for signs of life in the world,
when he feels bad, he goes to the library to read controver-
sial periodicals, because the hatred of liberals for conserva-
tives and vice versa "strikes me as one of the few signs of

life remaining in the world. This is another thing about
the world which is upsidedown: all the friendly and lik-
able people seem dead to me; only the haters seem alive."
(p. 95) So the world of the screen, perforce, takes over;
Marshal Dillon of *Gunsmoke*, for example, is a hero:
"This is no ordinary marshal. He is also a humanist."

> "It ain't nothing but a stinking Indian," says one of the
> killers. "You're wrong," says the marshal. "It is a human
> being." In the end he prevails upon the killers to spare the
> baby and even to have it baptized. The killers go out in a
> gruff manner and fetch the padre, a fellow who looks as
> much like the late H. B. Warner as it is possible for a man
> to look. (pp. 101–2)

Bolling's struggle to identify, to admire "right conduct"
and despise chicanery, is linked to a sense of the "malaise"
which, he thinks, the world is suffering. "The malaise is
the pain of loss. The world is lost to you, the world and
the people in it, and there remains only you and the world
and you no more able to be in the world than Banquo's
ghost." (p. 114) The "malaise" happens to you suddenly,
and when it does, it needs to be fought off. In his MG
sports car, he is immune to the malaise; as he and his
lovely "drum majorette of a secretary" travel toward the
Gulf, the malaise holds off. On the way, an accident with
a westbound green Ford, and Bolling is now "in solid"
with Sharon, as well as Bill Holden ever was in the films.
The world is a dream, broken in occasionally by Howard
Johnson restaurants, motels and the children's carnival.

A visit to his mother is followed by speculation upon
the meaning of God.

> Sometimes when she mentions God, it strikes me that
> my mother uses him as but one of the devices that come to
> hand in an outrageous man's world, to be put to work like
> all the rest in the one enterprise she has any use for: the
> canny management of the shocks of life. It is a bargain
> struck at the very beginning in which she settled for a
> general belittlement of everything, the good and the bad.
> (p. 133)

Instead of these locutions, Bolling depends upon the filmed world, which is marked by repetitions and rotations: "A rotation I define as the experiencing of the new beyond the expectation of the experiencing of the new." (p. 134) In other words, a lucky shot, a world suddenly opening up when one doesn't expect it. The trouble is that "when I awake, I awake in the grip of everydayness. Everydayness is the enemy. . . . Now nothing breaks it—but disaster. Only once in my life was the grip of everydayness broken: When I lay bleeding in a ditch." (p. 135)

It is obvious that *The Moviegoer* is an up-to-date, refurbished Baudelairean portrayal of *ennui, despair*, and the abyss. It is a comic fantasy, but throughout the narrator is fighting to individualize himself, fighting against the clichés of ambition, devoutness, order, and discretion, which he has heard all his life and which have no real meaning for him. Beginning with Chapter Four the novel takes a new turn: Bolling, fearful that his cousin Kate will commit suicide, agrees to travel with her to Chicago; he offers to marry her, but she calls the idea an "ingenious little scheme." (p. 177) The prospect of suicide, she says, is the "only thing that keeps me alive." (p. 179) She wants to believe in someone completely, then to do his bidding. Bolling engages in an imaginary conversation with Rory Calhoun about his good intentions and his failure. (p. 183) But before the malice sets in, in Chicago, he rushes to a movie house, "an Aztec mortuary of funeral urns and glyphs, thronged with the spirit-presence of another day, William Powell and George Brent and Patsy Kelly and Charley Chase, the best friends of my childhood," to see a movie, *The Young Philadelphians*, with Paul Newman, "an idealistic young fellow who is disillusioned and becomes cynical and calculating. But in the end he recovers his ideals." (p. 193) That was it about the movies; in the end, they recapture their ideals, and the memory of their conversions can be recaptured by seeing the movie again, in rerun.

Back in New Orleans, Bolling is severely scolded by his

aunt for the Chicago adventure. Her lecture to him is a
parody of rationally "good advice." The "other generation," trying to understand Bolling, comes out with words
only, and semi-slogans. They have listened to music together, read the *Crito*, had intelligent conversation about
goodness and truth and nobility. But where has she failed
him?

> I am silent.
> "Tell me where I have failed you."
> "You haven't." (p. 207)

But their friendship is over; the gap between them will
never be closed, and her brisk smile marks a close to her
mistaken ambitions for him.

On his thirtieth birthday, Bolling meditates upon "my
dark pilgrimage on this earth and knowing less than I ever
knew before, having learned only to recognize merde
when I see it . . ." (p. 208) All persons are humanists,
and "ninety-eight percent believe in God, and men are
dead, dead, dead; and the malaise has settled like a
fall-out . . ." (p. 209) The Epilogue cheats a bit. He and
Kate are married, he is to start in medical school in the
fall, and his aunt is fond of him again. But this is not
really a part of the novel, which is concerned with the
false labels and definitions the "humanists" have used and
the agonies caused by his not subscribing to their purposes; and, finally, his having run to the movies to find a
way of closing the abyss. In the end, he conducts a steady
monologue with Rory Calhoun concerning the virtues of
his case. But he is unable to sustain it, and must go to the
protection of his aunt's precise good will and the institution of marriage and science.

The Moviegoer is a remarkable use of the man who uses
the cinema world as a counter to the real one. The two
worlds do have points of contact, but ultimately the one is
unable to make up for the deficiencies of the other, especially since the movie world often has the same inadequacies, blown up. *The Last Gentleman* (1966) is a more
elaborate conception and surely an important work. Once

again it features the lost young man, Will Barrett, searching for forms and meanings and trying to "be good" as
nearly as he can see his way to it. He begins in New York,
with a fortune of $18,000, most of which he spends on
psychiatry. He is a maintenance engineer, works at night,
specializing in Temperature and Humidification Control;
during the day he scans the city landscape with a tele-
scope, "a wicked unlovely and purely useful thing." (p.
33) Barrett's malaise consists in attacks of *déja vu*, experiences of total recall, which shake and disturb him and
upset the pattern of present behavior. He wants to serve,
and before he has found his way to do so he will have
many strange adventures. If there is nothing wrong with
him, he says, then there is something wrong with the
world. (p. 78)

The key to Barrett's conduct is propriety; he is "the last
gentlemen." He is forever at the task of establishing his
credentials. (pp. 112–13) The effort to establish himself as
valid and authentic first takes him into Virginia, with
Forney Aiken, a white photographer who is going through
the South to do a "photographic essay" on the Negro; he
disguises as a Negro for the purpose. Of course this change
of appearance causes near riots, especially when Aiken
attempts to walk into his own house, in Levittown.

This is a foretaste. *The Last Gentlemen* is a picaresque
novel concerning the adventures of a subtly sincere person
who is trying to get into exact focus with present circumstance. Most of his travels through the South are with the
Vaught family, whom he first met in New York. In
Charlestown, South Carolina, he observes the pretty details of the past; "pretty wooden things, old and all
painted white, a thick-skinned decorous white, thick as
ship's paint, and presided over by the women." (p. 164)
He tries to define himself by loving Kitty ("her charms
and his arms"), but "she was too dutiful and athletic." (p.
166)

> Why is it not wonderful, he wondered, and when he
> leaned over again and embraced her in the sand, he know-
> ing without calculating the exact angle at which he might

lie over against her—about twenty degrees past the vertical—she miscalculated, misread him and moved slightly, yet unmistakably to get plainly and simply under him, then feeling the surprise in him stopped almost before she began. It was like correcting a misstep in dancing. (pp. 166–67)

He was the boy, and she was doing her best to do what a girl does.

Obviously, the arrangement isn't going to work; their actions are too much à la mode. Barrett is Percy's version of the twentieth-century *Candide*; that is, he is not optimistic, but rather *sincere*, a quality that will cause many difficulties along the way. As they move through Georgia they note the machines being used for cutting through a new freeway: "The whole South throbbed like a Diesel." (p. 169) Kitty comes at him like a Diesel locomotive, and it doesn't work out. The South he returns to is different from the one he had left: "more and more cars which had Confederate plates on the front bumper and plastic Christs on the dashboard." (p. 186) The *déja vus* now compete with the raw, jangling present South.

The Vaught castle in Georgia is obviously a major eyesore symbol of the new South. It fronts on a golf course and is made of purplish bricks, "beam-in-plaster gables and a fat Norman tower and casement windows with panes of bottle glass." (p. 189) As Mr. Vaught says, it's a good place "to live and collect one's thoughts." (p. 191) Here Will Barrett meets Sutter, the archdemon, cynic, a character from an imitation of a Dostoevsky novel. He had been a doctor once, and one of his patients had died because of a theory Sutter had had about illness and well-being; he has retired from the profession since. (p. 219) It is Sutter who asks all the disturbing questions: Do you believe in God? Do you think God entered history? How do you define a gentleman? (p. 221) Especially under the influence of the last question, Barrett's suffers a *déja vu* which encompasses his father's views of and relations to Negroes. Each time he tries to make a "sensible settlement" of his affairs (marrying Kitty, taking over a

position in Vaught's Chevrolet agency, etc.), a *déja vu*
assaults him. This idea, of the *déja vu* interfering with too
easy a solution of the present, is like Bolling's problems in
The Moviegoer, where eventually communication with
Rory Calhoun of the film world breaks down.

Sutter's notebooks or "Casebooks" carry the philosophical burden the rest of the way. "I am the only sincere
American," he announces in one entry.

> Soap opera is overtly decent and covertly lewd. The Ameri-
> can theatre is overtly lewd and covertly homosexual. I am
> overtly heterosexual and overtly lewd. I am therefore the
> only sincere American. (p. 293)

Further observations concern the "new South." The
Southern businessman is the new Adam, but "the truth of
it is, you were pleased because you talked the local Coca-
Cola distributor into giving you a new gym." (p. 308)
Sutter acts as a disturbing influence on Barrett; there are
points upon which they agree, but his cynicism gives
Barrett a jolt. Barrett's trouble is that he has had a liberal,
philosophical father, who knew the right literary allusion
for an occasion, while Sutter (like the devil) can quote
scriptures to his advantage as well. They are two generations of intellectual, and Barrett has to decide between
them. He used to walk with his father, he remembers,
"and speak of the galaxies and of the expanding universe
and take pleasure in the insignificance of man in the great
lonely universe. His father would recite 'Dover Beach,'
setting his jaw askew and wagging his head like F.D.R."
(p. 309) His trouble, writes Sutter, is "that he wants to
know what his trouble is. . . . That is to say: he wishes to
cling to his transcendence and to locate a fellow tran-
scender (e.g., me) who will tell him how to traffic with
immanence . . ." (p. 353) This is an exact description of
Barrett's dilemma, but it doesn't explain Sutter's.

Sutter's points of view and Barrett's *déja vus* tend to
take over the novel, the plot of which concerns the
Vaught son, Jamie, who is in Barrett's care. Sutter "steals"
him, drives him to Santa Fe, where he appears about to

die. Barrett faces Sutter in the hospital, annoying him and pressing home the moral point of his reasons for taking him out west. The two opponents now face each other with hostility.

> "Violence is bad."
> "Violence is not good."
> "It is better to make love to one's wife then to monkey around with a lot of women."
> "A lot better."
> "I am sure I am right."
> "You are right." (p. 385)

This exchange is a parody catechism of the most superficial liberal virtues, and both Sutter and Barrett are aware that it is worthless. But Barrett confesses that he needs Sutter, to correct him in his "gentlemanliness," to be there always as a cynical guard against excessive, unwanted goodness. The gentleman needs the cynic, the skeptic, to watch over him.

This is as much as Percy's second novel does; but, in its exploration of the man of good will, it scores many points. Essentially, Barrett is disturbed by the same world that troubles Bolling—a world of chaos and villainy and accident that just isn't properly available to easy definition. Bolling has recourse to the "good guys" in the movies and on television, but eventually he has to give them up. He suffers from malaise, which strikes him without warning. Barrett *wants* the old clichés to work; but in the end he admits that they are a hindrance to a realistic adjustment to the world as it is: The stinks, the vulgarities, the pompousness, all of the defects that Sutter had noticed long before.

v

Reynolds Price has from the beginning been hailed as a special product of Southern writing. He has rewarded expectations with three books of fiction: the novel, *A Long and Happy Life* (1962); the short stories, *The Names and Faces of Heroes* (1963); and the novel, *A*

Generous Man (1966).[25] They are all concerned with the
Mustian family and assorted relatives, friends, and townspeople. In the first novel, Rosacoke Mustian consummates
an eight-year-long love of Wesley Beavers one night in the
broomstraw meadows, because she wanted so much to
give of herself and can think of no better way—only to
discover (or so she thinks) that Wesley is accepting the
gift perfunctorily (he even thanks a "Mae" from out of
his past, unconsciously, for the favor). A period of grim
waiting follows, with Rosacoke adamantly refusing further
invitations. Then she tells him she is expecting his child;
he proposes they go to Dillon, North Carolina, to get
married, and she decides finally it is "her duty" as well as
his, as well as her wish. Apparently with this decision
(*Life*, p. 195), the desire for "a long and happy life"
which the novel has semi-ironically announced in its title,
has been entirely denied, and Rosa has to settle for the
risks and haphazard joys of an ordinary marriage, without
the extraordinary pleasures her dreams have projected.

The reality will fall far short of the ideal. There is the
risk of semipoverty; there is the risk that Wesley will
follow in the pattern of her father (who had lost his
control and become a sudden drunk, until one night,
when he walked straight up the road into an oncoming
truck). And of course there is the pregnancy, which points
at "her fault." Her gift becomes her act becomes "her
fault." The novel is a marvel of vital and other kinds of
statistics. It opens with a funeral, which is interrupted by
a picnic, itself a vital statistic of sorts; Rosacoke's sister has
a stillborn child, and her husband—distraught by the general and the implicit slurs such an event suggests concerning his manhood—walks out of the house; but he returns,
having come into the world equipped more sternly than
Rosa's father had been. There is the fetching scene of the
very old and the very wealthy Mr. Isaac being attended
solicitously by the Negro Sammy.

The crucial event is the concluding one (the ironies are
of course very much on the surface): Rosacoke is dele-
gated to watch the eight-month-old Frederick Gupton,

who is the Christchild in the Christmas pageant; she has
to pick him up as Wesley approaches (Wesley plays one
of the Wise Men). So she inadvertently plays the role of
the Virgin Mary, as indeed she has in life, "giving herself"
as a form of sacrificial grace, a gesture of a redeeming
faith. She seems disillusioned, though resigned at the end
to the necessities that life imposes upon her.

This was a first book, by an obviously talented young
man. It is not an entirely successful book, nor is it entirely
well communicated.[26] If there is a failure, it is in the
occasional oversimplification, Price making decisions
about what his fictional world should be before the world
has been fully represented. Rosacoke comes through as a
bemused and whimsical creature; we are inclined to nod
with approval over her final decision, without really being
sure that it represents any maturity on her part, or any
release from adolescent impulse. If we stay on her level of
consciousness, then the novel is a minor success. Price has
a talent for communicating by means of style in terms of
his heroine's own emotional nature, a talent shared by
such writers as Eudora Welty and Flannery O'Connor.
The seven stories of *The Names and Faces of Heroes* are
concerned with the same settings and with many of the
same people. In the first, "A Chain of Love" (pp. 3–43),
four of them appear. "Papa" of the story is Rosacoke's
grandfather, and he is also much in evidence as well in the
second novel, *A Generous Man*.

Like *A Long and Happy Life*, these stories resemble in
style and type of incident those of Eudora Welty more
than the work of Faulkner or Miss Porter. The first story is
located in the hospital where Rato is confined. In her vigil
in the hospital Rosacoke feels that she should say something to the people on their hospital beds, "because you
felt for them, because you hadn't ever been that sick or
that old or that alone in all your life and because you
wished they hadn't been either." (pp. 23–24). The wait in
the hospital is well represented: waiting for something,
you didn't know what, "but the only thing happened was,
time made noise in a clock somewhere way off." (p. 26)

And Rosacoke has thoughts of someone's dying: where does he go when he dies? The Phelps boy, who had been rescued from drowning, didn't care to say, maintaining it was a secret between him and Jesus. She thinks of him as someone who had seen Hell "with his own eyes and had lived to tell the tale." (p. 28)

The stories are all involved in courtships and weddings, anniversaries and disappointments. "The Anniversary" (pp. 64–92) presents Miss Lilian Belle's past: she had planned a wedding, which was set for September 15, in the hope that it would be cooler then and that the last roses could still be used. But her fiancé dies in an accident before the date, so that instead of a small wedding, there is a small burial. "Troubled Sleep" (pp. 93–109) presents a narrator who is only nine years old, caught in the woods, calling out for help. The one word, "Help!" "held out like a hard pear I could take or leave." (p. 94)

> When they missed us from our bed and my father came out at midnight to lead us home, walking straight as any judge to the bench, he found us in that secret place where he knew we were, and all he could see, he smiled at—me in troubled sleep in the full moon still and Falc dark and gone like he didn't mean to return, but in each other's arms at least and breathing slow. (p. 109)

"Uncle Grant" (pp. 110–37) presents a new point of view. Reynolds Price, in Oxford, England, comes upon a picture of the head of Amenhotep iv and is reminded of "Uncle Grant," Grant Terry, born about 1865 and "named for a general his parents heard of who set them free." (p. 113) Uncle Grant was Price's companion and the family gardener, a miracle at making things grow; he lasted until ninety, though of course toward the end he grew more and more helpless. When they last saw each other Uncle Grant had told him he would see Price in heaven—his last joke, if it was a joke: "whoever it was on, it was not on him." (p. 137) In the title story the narrator looks back upon the time when he was nine, thinks of his great love for his father: "My eyes stay blind and I think what I know, 'I love you tonight more than all my life before'—think it in *my* natural voice." He is searching for the face of *his* hero; his minister had preached that "When you find what your main lack is, seek that in some great man." (p. 140) When you find him, "chin yourself on his example and you will be a man before you need a razor." (p. 141) He studies his father as the man who might be able to compensate for all *his* faults. He appeals to Jesus to help him, and the image of Jesus dissolves into his father, sitting next to him. "They did not separate us tonight. We finished alive, together, whole, this one more time." (p. 178)

A Generous Man is the story of Milo Mustian; it is more fanciful than the earlier two books, though concerned once again with the same family. Milo is now in his fifteenth year, in the process of growing up. The major adventure is a search for Milo's brother Rato (Horatio), who is himself searching for his dog, Philip, who is chasing a 20-foot, 280-pound python. The novel begins in these terms; it will have to be comical, since it is too absurd to be taken seriously. He is also alive to Rosacoke, younger than he (she is only eleven), and to his grandfather and his mother. He has been growing apart from his sister; "this year had rammed him beyond her." (p. 30) The scene at the vet's office, where Rato's dog is taken for the diagnosis of a mysterious illness, is a fine comical episode. But the great snake, named Death, from a carnival nearby, is to take over from all of them.

The sheriff gathers a posse to find the snake, and Milo is deputized to help. He's had a full life, but "this job is the height of my life." (p. 108) Milo's prayers are for three things: "Let me find Rato, let me find Death, then let me take my ease on some girl." (p. 110) The posse comes upon a still, a digression, and Milo is quite undone by the liquor. He goes on to the sheriff's house and encounters his wife, who faints upon seeing him, mistaking him for someone else (or pretending to do so); the affair is surrounded by story and legend, concerning a young man whom she had known years ago and waited for ever since, who looks exactly like Milo.

Once more on the chase, he is attacked by the python,

while the people stand around offering suitable commentary. Whether this is a dream or not is not clear. For a while, the family despairs that Rato is dead; Milo now thinks of himself as "the man" in the house. The novel is only ostensibly about the great snake chase, though that certainly causes more than one ripple on its surface; it is, mainly, about Milo's move toward manhood. He will have to "take charge" if Rato is actually dead. He is immensely impressed by the coming to manhood he thinks he has experienced, and he turns to Lois Provo, his girl, to explain it all to her:

> He turned again from her to the lantern—flame as steady as hammered iron—and waited tensely for the knowledge to gather, the wounds and visions of three clear days to narrow the gap between his eyes behind his skull, transform into words. And he clamped his eyes to force the conversion, but only colors came—the reds and purples of his own thick blood as it thinned in his eyelids, received the light—no word, not one. (p. 270)

But the seriousness of the occasion is dissipated when Rato appears on the scene, thus relieving Milo, temporarily at least, from the grave and mature responsibilities he thought he was going to have.

This is a comic novel. Milo's reactions are only occasionally to be respected; mostly, they are to be condoned and indulged. Reviewing it in the *New Republic*, John Wain complained vigorously that it was imitative, that it "smells of the lamp." [27] He then proceeded to review Price's career: *A Long and Happy Life* he described as "Southern" in the sense that "we, the rest of the world, have long since come to understand the term. It deals with simple characters; it describes a rural setting and rather consciously old-fashioned ways. It is also written in a prose that we may call stylized, if we wish to be kind, or affected, if we feel it necessary to be astringent; it has the *faux-naif* quality that seems to hang round Southern writing." (p. 31) Wain insists upon linking Price's work with Faulkner's, though the association is not nearly so great as with other Southern writers. ". . . I felt a vague disquiet at the book's closeness to Faulkner, whose irritating mannerisms are so much more imitable than his moral and imaginative largeness . . ." (p. 32)

Wain's points are off the mark more often than not. There is an assumption that Price has "taken up" the rural life of the South in *A Generous Man* because "of its picturesque qualities. It offers a ready-made source of color and character; in American writing, it occupies exactly the same place as books about Ireland occupy in English writing." Perhaps it is not too late, he concludes, to remind Price "that Faulkner's books have already been written, and that, which ever way you look at it, one Yoknapatawpha County is enough." (p. 33) The point of resemblance is not Faulkner, but (if at all) Miss Welty and Miss O'Connor. As for the preoccupation with the Mustian family, I shouldn't think that it was necessarily a fault. If anything, Price may be accused of never quite sorting out his basic attitudes toward his characters. When they are not of advanced ages (like "Papa") and therefore in a reduced sense "rejuvenated," they are teenagers. What we get from them is a certain preciousness, a certain daintiness and delicacy, which is played upon by a fine irony. In order to overcome the monotony of this impression, in *A Generous Man* he has introduced a fabulous tale, of a search for a boy seeking his dog seeking an enormous snake, and imports complications about Thomas Ryden, kidnaper and soldier and lover. The result is a fantasy which superintends the young hero's sense of growing up. All of these matters he communicates quite fully and quite well.

WILLIAM STYRON:
       THE METAPHYSICAL HURT

WHILE William Styron has quite correctly refused to be
called a "Southern writer," in an interview for the *Paris
Review* he did admit that the South supplies "wonderful
material."

> Take, for instance, the conflict between the ordered Protes-
> tant tradition, the fundamentalism based on the Old Testa-
> ment, and the twentieth century—movies, cars, television.
> The poetic juxtapositions you find in this conflict—a crazy
> colored preacher howling those tremendously moving verses
> from Isaiah 40, while riding around in a maroon Packard.
> It's wonderful stuff and comparatively new, too, which is
> perhaps why the renaissance of Southern writing coincided
> with these last few decades of the machine age.[1]

It is futile to stir up the old clichés about "decadence,"
"Southern tradition," the "Southern model," etc.[2] Styron
has better and larger fish to fry. He is, above all, concerned
with a basic and timeless issue, though it surely has its
place in twentieth-century literature.

It is, in brief, the problem of believing, the desperate
necessity for having the "courage to be." Almost all of his
fiction poses violence against the human power to endure
it and to "take hold of himself" in spite of it. The pathos
of his creatures, when it is not directly the result of
organizational absurdity,[3] comes from a psychological failure, a "confusion," a situation in which the character,
trying to meet an awkward human situation, makes it
worse and (almost invariably) retreats clumsily or despair-
ingly from it.

Writing to the *Paris Review* (of which he has been an Advisory Editor) for its first issue, on the ever-present questions of "the times" (*are* they worthy, or *do* they promise good literature, etc.), Styron said:

> I still maintain that the times get precisely the literature that they deserve, and that if the writing is gloomy the gloom is not so much inherent in the literature as in the times. . . . The writer will be dead before anyone can judge him—but he *must* go on writing, reflecting disorder, defeat, despair, should that be all he sees at the moment, but ever searching for the elusive love, joy and hope— qualities which, as in the act of life itself, are best when they have to be struggled for, and are not commonly come by with much ease, either by a critic's formula or by a critic's yearning. . . .[4]

There is nothing very complicated about this. It is a fairly simple set of human explorations. In a way, it is a twentieth-century restatement of Baudelaire's "Le Gouffre." Only here, in Styron's fiction, it takes on a far less subjective, isolative character. Lack of belief causes great cracks in the human landscape: and men look, desperate and afraid, across them at each other. Most of what they do has the character of trying to heal the wound, close the gap, but by means of ordinary secular devices. Alcohol has an important role in the lives of Styron's characters, but it is not a way of closing the fissure; it temporarily makes things *appear* improved, but it may ultimately lead to disaster. It is simply not a surrogate of God, though God's absence is surely responsible for the increase of its use.

I do not mean to suggest that Styron inhabits or has created a simple-minded world. It is perhaps the most difficult feat of all, this one of asserting not only the pre-eminence of values (love, joy, and hope [5]) but of creating meaningful situations in which men and women struggle to gain them, or even to understand them. The "modernness" of Styron's world, then, is not related to nihilism, but to humiliation, and to struggle: the ghastly struggle just to *assert* one's humanness, to get over the barriers to understanding, to clear one's personality of obsessions. Another way of putting it is that the Styron hero is trying for a clear view and a steady hand, like the hand of Cass Kinsolving *after* he has freed himself of the imprisonment within despair and within the obsessive indulgences used temporarily to combat it.[6]

ii

Styron's minor prose is largely confined to asserting these essentials, as though the essays and sketches were a clearinghouse, to provide the novels a freer range of observation and action. The brief sketch on the funeral of William Faulkner, in *Life* magazine of July 20, 1962, puts a cap upon the lot; he speaks reverently, not only of his dead hero, but of the very substance and center of Yoknapatawpha County: the famous square in downtown Oxford, the courthouse and jail, the statue of the Confederate soldier.[7] Even a very early short story, "The Long Dark Road," selected by his teacher, William Blackburn, for inclusion in a Duke University anthology, concerns one of those calamitous explosions of human irrationality (in this case, a lynching) which Styron repeatedly described afterward in his two major novels.[8] His essays include one against capital punishment, in which he puzzles over why it is that the poor are condemned so much more often than the rest, and meditates upon "the soul" of the victim, which "will have been already so diminished by our own humanity" by the time it is "taken."[9]

The Long March gives an insight into the simplest variant of Styron's moral speculation.[10] If we assume that the human creature deserves (or can rise to) dignity and even nobility, but is often the victim of accident and absurdity, *The Long March* illustrates our assumption with the simplicity of a blackboard demonstration. As the novel opens we see, "in the blaze of a cloudless Carolina summer," in a Marine training camp,

> What was left of eight dead boys [which] lay strewn about the landscape, among the poison ivy and the pine needles and loblolly saplings. . . . (p. 3)

A propos only of the general absurdity of this military world, the "bone, gut, and dangling tissue" point to a haphazard regime, and even to a mad one; at least, its absurdity is a compound of accidental and humanly willed disasters.

In subsequent events, the Colonel (Templeton) of the Marine troop orders his men on a 36-mile hike, to prove nothing at all except that his man can and should walk the distance. Lieutenant Culver, the novel's hero, is also its center, because he is the only one whose personality is seen in more than one dimension. There is a phrase from Haydn, recalled from a brief peacetime stretch in Washington Square, with a wife, a cat, and a record player, which haunts his mind throughout and is apparently to remind one of a saner world beyond this spectral and weird military enclosure. The Haydn plays a role roughly similar to a recording of Mozart's *Don Giovanni* in *Set This House on Fire*, which Kinsolving uses to "blast" the "ghosts" of his neighbors in Sambuco. In any case, it is one of Styron's frequent insertions from the "cultivated world" which always makes one wonder if they are necessary.

Styron is very sophisticated and erudite; he will break in with a Haydn phrase or a quotation from *Oedipus at Colonus*, to set the unwary on an unnecessary search for a "Waste Land" type of significance.[11] Here, in *The Long March*, the references are of course used with a stark simplicity. The clarity and beauty of the Haydn phrase contrast with the true absurdity of the hot, sticky North Carolina scene. The central victim of its absurdity is Captain Mannix, a friend of Culver's who persists beyond all but his human endurance to fulfill the Colonel's absurd orders.

> [His persistence] lent to his face . . . an aspect of deep, almost prayerfully passionate concentration—eyes thrown skyward and lips fluttering feverishly in pain—so that if one did not know he was in agony one might imagine that he was a communicant in rapture, offering up breaths of hot desire to the heavens. . . . (*March*, pp. 113–14)

Aside from the evidence this passage offers of Styron's close study of Faulkner's style,[12] it is a statement concerning the world of the absurd. Mannix does not defy its absurdity; he simply goes about to prove that he can meet its terms, and becomes in the end a reduced figure as a result of his efforts. Perhaps, by way of extenuation, it should be said that the terms here are extraordinarily simple. Despite the fact that this world is absurd, there are few problems of communication here. It is not the military world that usually bothers Styron's persons, but the civilian world living in the shadow of a war, a "bomb," and, principally, in a circumstance that permits no easy belief.

iii

It is this combination of appalling and threatening circumstances that makes *Lie Down in Darkness* [13] so sad a novel. Throughout the interior monologue (pp. 335–86) of young Peyton Loftis, the atom bomb just dropped on Hiroshima appears as a menacing minor overtone. This is not a war novel, however; nor is it a novel devoted to diagnoses of civilians hurt by neurosis-inducing fright or guilt. It is, in fact, a "witness novel," that testifies to a special depth of human suffering and struggle. It is, as such, one of the representative novels of the 1950's and 1960's: the postwar novel of anxiety *and* manners, to which American Jewish novelists have made so substantial a contribution. There is a point at which the total impact of unhappiness is so great that one has the impression that it is God's will it should be so. But this is not true. The agony is not that of sheer victimization. Superficially, it is set off by a husband and wife who are incompatible and whose sins are visited upon their child.[14] Once again superficially, the novel poses a morality and religion inadequate to the pressure and demands made upon them by the modern world. At any rate, the noises and smells of Port Warwick,[15] Virginia, are sufficiently strong to emphasize the fact that industry has invaded a world accustomed to being governed by a fairly slow, "closed" tradition and manners.

I think it is a mistake to assume that *Darkness* is simply a study of "decadence" or "degeneration," two terms that have been too easily applied to both Styron and Faulkner. They do not explain anything. Far from being what Elizabeth Janeway says they are, "hardly conscious enough to be decadent," [16] the three Loftises are all too alive to the pressures and conditions that continue to get in the way of their understanding each other. The agony of human error is so great that there is no real center of blame. Helen Loftis may at times be thought as the root source; and at times her narrow, religiously excused sentiments toward pleasure and SIN (as she capitalizes it) do appear responsible. But Milton Loftis is deeply at fault, in having taken to drink and adultery too quickly, as though they were nostrums available on the medicine shelf. And, finally, Peyton Loftis, alone in Manhattan, rejected by her husband whom she has quite openly "deceived," is both culpable and pitiful. In short, one comes eventually to the conclusion—as happens often in O'Neill plays—that no one is either totally guilty or blameless; that there is a "fate," terribly and pathetically human, that hovers over the novel.

In his not having settled for easy answers, his refusal simply to settle for "decadence" or "Southern *malaise*" as an explanation of his Loftises, Styron has struggled toward a great achievement in *Darkness*. Once again, there is a complement of "erudite" references; this time, however, they are largely effective. The epigraph gives us the cue for the title, which is from Sir Thomas Browne's *Urn Burial*:

> . . . since our longest sun sets at right descencions, and makes but winter arches, and therefore it cannot be long before we lie down in darkness, and have our light in ashes. . .

The last words are repeated at the end of Peyton's monologue, as she prepares to commit suicide:

> . . . Perhaps I shall rise at another time, though I lie down in darkness and have my light in ashes. . . . (p. 386) [17]

Lie Down in Darkness, as its title directs it to be, is concerned with human mortality, with the relentless drive of the death wish, which is underscored, of course, by a sense of almost total hopelessness. It is significant that the young Peyton, in the "present scene" of Port Warwick of 1945, is dead; we see her alive only in the past. In fact, we are aware of death in her and working in her in several ways: the coffin itself, of whose contents her father desperately tries to avoid imagining; before that, the body buried in Potter's Field, on Hart's Island, and claimed by her distraught husband of a few months and his friend; before that, death in her body (the womb painfully resists its function in Peyton's several affairs) as she fearfully walks the streets of Manhattan, vainly seeking the forgiveness of her husband, and fighting the cynical view of a mechanical, atomic world. And we may go back, almost to the beginning of her life, when the seeds of death are planted, as she reacts to the sheer hopelessness of her parents' incompatibility and to the almost incestuous tenderness with which her father treats her, by way of overcompensating for the coldness and emptiness of his married life.

Darkness is so constructed that we are forever beholding the fact of death; the coffin holding Peyton's "remains," present before us, poses simply the question "Why did she die?" For, as the epigraph offers us no hope of immortality and bids us prepare for our own death, the corpse of an eighteen-year-old girl is an ever-present *memento mori*.

There are many answers to the question, and none. Peyton killed herself, or did her father, in his last view of her, frighten her into a pact with death? As she prepares to leave Port Warwick with her husband (as it is, her last time in her birthplace alive) she speaks desperately and angrily of

> ". . . Daddy! He's had so much that was good in him, but it was all wasted. He wasn't man enough to stand up and make decisions and all the rest. . . . Aren't things bad enough in the world without having him crawl back to that idiot? . . ." (*Darkness*, p. 317)

The poignancy of these random and angry remarks is not realized until we read the interior monologue preceding the suicide. Peyton has finally had to realize that her father is and will be no protection for her, that she must expose herself to life, alone, which means going, naked, to death.

For *Darkness* is, much of the way, a story of ordinary middle-class incompatibility and adultery: "ordinary," because the description of it is mean, tawdry, and without hope. Neither husband nor wife is heroic in any of it, though for a short time he appears in one of those interludes of fidelity and good intentions. It is also, and in close relationship to its other function, a novel which concerns the modern sensibility's frantic compulsions, its all but helpless drive toward self-destruction. When it is over, Milton Loftis, in his fifties and on the way to the funeral of his only remaining child, rushes into the rain away from his wife and his mistress, acknowledging for the first time *le néant* in all of its emptiness:

> Loftis pulled Helen about so that she faced him and began to choke her. "God damn you!" he yelled, "If I can't have . . . then you . . . nothing!"
> "People!" Carey [the minister] cried. "People! People!" He couldn't move.
> "Die, damn you, die!"
>
> . . . .
>
> The last [Carey] saw of him was his retreating back, amid all the wind and rain, as he hustled on, bounding past wreaths and boxwood and over tombstones, toward the highway.
> Then Helen steadied herself against Carey, and she pressed her head next to the wall. "Peyton," she said, "Oh, God, Peyton. My child. Nothing! Nothing! Nothing! Nothing!" (*Darkness*, pp. 388–89)

The full impact of this passage can come only after a careful reading of the entire novel. There is truly "Nothing!" left. Milton and Helen Loftis finally face this prospect, Helen ironically in the presence of her minister, whose pitifully futile attempts to bring her the solaces of religion now end in a pathetic figure, quite unable to give her the desperately needed words of God's grace. The stresses and strains are all in the present, as are the ironic meanings of the stench, the noise, the burial ground, and the Negro revival.[18] Their importance can be sensed, however, only in the past. Through the history of their marriage, and especially in the attractive upper middle-class residential community overlooking the bay, the move toward the hopeless conclusion is inevitable; but its inevitability doesn't always "show." There are times of comparative peace, when both husband and wife seem willing to give in a little.

Nevertheless, three major conditions hover always on the edge of their lives, and make for the pathos of the final hours: Helen's religion (or, her spiteful and even pitiful uses of it); Milton's drinking, which he uses as an easy escape from acknowledging the pathetic sadness of their fate; and Peyton's self-indulgent dependence upon an all but incestuous relationship with her father. Perhaps Styron is saying: These people do not deserve a better fate. Or he may be saying: they are ineluctably fated to end as they do. But beyond any "naturalistic" or "fatalistic" view of them he sees them as persons engaged in pitifully trying to save themselves, or each other, from a fate they are somehow not able to forestall. As he himself said, to David Dempsey:

> I wanted to tell the story of four tragically fated people, one of them [Maudie] the innocent victim of the others. It was important to me that I write about this thing, but I can't tell you why. I didn't conceive it, directly at any rate, as a contemporary statement of any kind. The symbols are there, I suppose, but to me the important thing was the story.[19]

It is, of course, *not* a "contemporary statement," except in the limited sense that industrial ugliness intrudes upon the Loftis world, and the explosion of the Hiroshima bomb sounds menacingly in the distance during Peyton's tragic last day in New York City. The great achievement of *Darkness* is that it is a *universal* situation. There is nothing peculiarly Southern, or even especially characteristic of the "U.S.A." in the novel. It is a bit too much the melodrama to be called a tragedy. Yet the images of a death hovering over life are sufficiently clearly there, to make the whole comparable to the seventeenth century of *Urn Burial*, and of John Donne's sermons.

In short, *Darkness* poses the metaphysical problem of death in a setting in which there is insufficient accommodation for it. The ambiguities of a love and a happiness that seem always beyond reach, for one reason or another; the further perplexities of a man who loves too much, too earnestly, and too vainly: these are novelistic meditations not unlike the poetic and religious meditations typified by the novel's epigraph.

They say a number of things: for one, that we are all doomed; that our lives are but a preparing for death; most importantly, that we somehow (without overtly wishing to, but nevertheless, as if compulsively) help our own way toward self-destruction. Styron is saying that *any* inducement to neurotic behavior, any psychological self-flagellation, is suicidal. The most tragically compelling question at the novel's end is which of the three is the most doomed: Peyton, whose body has been dug up from Potter's Field; Milton, who walks away from her grave crying out "Nothing!" like a middle-class excommunicated King Lear; or Helen, who turns away from the minister of her faith, to repeat the "Nothing!" several times to a blank wall? They are akin in their being doomed, in their having lived a life that somehow has unavoidably led to their doom, in their willing their doom by not acting (perhaps, by not being able to act) to prevent it.

Styron avoids a total surrender to melodrama in several ways. One of these is style. One of the qualities that distinguish writers of Styron's generation from their predecessors of the 1920's is that, for Styron's contemporaries, style actually *does* function to qualify life. Perhaps this is because, most of the time at least, our younger novelists must somehow always "rescue" their work from naturalism and its nihilist metaphysics. They somehow have to improvise their own definitions of evil, their own theological metaphors. So, at crucial points, their characters are moral heroes, or moral clowns, or both.

Saul Bellow's Tommy Wilhelm, weeping desperately at a funeral of someone he has never known alive, at the end of his remarkable story, *Seize the Day* (1956), is an excellent case in point. The fact is that Loftis, no less and no more than his contemporary *personae*, improvises definitions as he invents poses to meet the terrible abysses left in their own society by the abject but somehow comprehensible failure of institutional religion to give protection in extreme crises. These circumstances, it seems to me, make for the kind of tragic failure that we see in this first of Styron's two great novels. Death hovers over the Loftis family from beginning to end; it is through death that we see their lives, as though we too were following the hearse, or waiting for the driver to repair its several mechanical failures, and steadily looking back on the scene of their tragic and impotent lives.

I don't believe that Styron intends the "Daddy Faith" episode at the novel's end to serve the same purpose as does Dilsey's Easter Sunday service in Faulkner's *The Sound and the Fury*. The aesthetic "competence" of Dilsey as a character, and the degree of Faulkner's preparing her for her culminating scene are both more acceptable in terms of the Compson débâcle. Besides, the Compson gallery is much more varied. There is very little to go on, for example, when we try to compare Milton Loftis with Quentin Compson's father. Both drink steadily; each is undoubtedly disillusioned with his marriage; the attitude of each has a strong influence on his children. But these are surface resemblances. Styron has earned the right to his own novel.

iv

Set This House on Fire bears a relationship to *Darkness* as an epic resembles a "tragedy of manners." Neither term quite successfully defines either novel, but there is an extensiveness of scope and scene in *House*, a largeness of ambition, that do not seem relevant to *Darkness*. The suggestiveness of the title is similarly involved in seventeenth-century metaphysics. This time, the source is John Donne's sermon "To the Earle of Carlile, and his Company, at Sion." In Styron's use of it, in his ambitious epigraph, it reads partly as follows:

> . . . God, who, when he could not get into me, by standing, by knocking . . . hath applied his judgements, and shaked the house, this body, with agues and palsies, and set this house on fire, with fevers and calentures, and frighted the Master of the house, my soule, with horrors, and heavy apprehensions, and so made an entrance into me. . . .[20]

In identifying both his major novels with seventeenth-century texts, Styron is in a sense also identifying them with the twentieth century: for in their contexts, he sees strong resemblances between the two centuries,[21] at least within the limits of certain basic meditations upon "last things."

House can of course superficially be seen as a conflict between the country bumpkin and the millionaire, but this theme dissolves into farce if pushed too hard. It is true that Cass Kinsolving is in the power of Mason Flagg; their names are also significantly involved, as is that of Peter Leverett, the narrator of Part One, and the listener of Part Two.[22] There is no doubt that Kinsolving is the hero of the novel, as Flagg is its villain. Both tower over everybody else in the novel, so that the next to final event in Sambuco, Italy (Kinsolving's killing of Flagg by forcing him over the cliff on the approach to a village beyond) is a struggle of giants. The real struggle is not the physical one, but Cass's struggle within himself. Flagg is indispensable to that struggle, of course: as he pushes Cass's weaknesses to the point of ridicule, he also provides the means of release from them.

Cass must be considered the hero of *House*; Peter Leverett says, "It is certainly not myself." (*House*, p. 4) In fact, Leverett is primarily designed to be observer and listener; even his hateful lashing out at Mason Flagg appears to be only an "observation," after all. Leverett is almost "computer-machine" American: "I am white, Protestant, Anglo-Saxon, Virginia-bred, just past thirty,[23] tolerable enough looking though possessing no romantic glint or cast, given to orderly habits, more than commonly inquisitive, and strongly sexed—though this is a conceit peculiar to all normal young men." (pp. 4–5) He is set up, first, to be attracted (because of an admiration of his apparent superiority) to Mason Flagg; then, to be repelled by him, as he slowly gathers in "counter" impressions; then, to be overwhelmed by Cass's pathetic status; finally, to be committed irrevocably to Cass's triumph over both Flagg and his own inner weaknesses. Leverett is also designed to communicate all of these facts without drawing attention to himself, despite the fact that he grows morally from step to step of the novel's progress.

Leverett is, in short, a "stamped out" model, a pigmy observing the struggles of giants. Since he has had no real temptations in his life, he has had to make neither compromises nor progress. Or, if there *is* progress in him, it is not interesting. What *is* of interest is the way Styron maneuvers him in both time and space. Only in Leverett's past is there a Mason Flagg: Cass's involvement with him occurs in the Sambuco "present," and this fact is of some importance to the novel's meaning. The "Thing" against which Cass struggles *didn't* start with Flagg, as he says to Peter; it started far back, in childhood, in youth, in The War, and *in himself*. To call him "villain" is not to say that he was evil. To Cass, he was "just scum." ". . . Beast, bastard, crook, and viper. But the guilt is not his! . . ." (*House*, p. 249)

Part of this strange "absolution" has to do with the *roman policier* aspect of *House*: Flagg did not kill Francesca, though he did rape her and did leave her half-dead; the village half-wit, Saverio, completed the job. But Cass's killing Flagg *did* take place and is of the essence. In killing him, Cass destroyed the nastiness inside him: the meanness which Michel Butor strangely calls "la condition américaine," as he calls the novel an "allégorie" of this condition and of "une invitation à la surmonter. . . ." [24] Whether it was "American" or not, Cass did triumph over a "something" within him that had (in affecting his mien) frightened prostitutes in Paris, driven him to thoughts of murder and suicide, and led to prodigious feats of drunkenness, the cost of which, for some weeks, led to a bondage to the arrogant "scum," Mason Flagg.

If anything, the idea of the millionaire's son, with an overly indulgent mother, an abundantly fertile imagination,[25] an extraordinary interest in sex (associated with a tendency toward impotence), is a legitimate one. But this fact does not make *House* "une allégorie de la condition américaine . . ." [26] The story of Mason Flagg is one of inventive nastiness; he is like Fitzgerald's Tom Buchanan, who, having played football at Yale, in middle age "drifted here and there unrestfully wherever people played polo and were rich together." [27] But while Buchanan is almost sullenly rich, Flagg takes advantage of his position almost creatively, certainly with verve and *esprit*. Peter Leverett refers in one place to him in "the dual role of daytime squire and nighttime nihilist." (*House*, p. 158) It is true that the strategies and the energy that go into the creation and the satisfaction of his whims are prodigious.

That they lead eventually to Flagg's being the Mephistophelean playboy, the archangel of all anti-christs, is true, and important; because by the time Cass Kinsolving confronts him (despite Cass's disclaimers) he needs a worthy antagonist. For, if we go back, we must remember that the "Thing," this *"quelque chose comme ça"* that was destroying Cass's soul and causing him to destroy his body, had started early and grown huge before he finally projected it upon his enemy and, in a traumatic crisis, expelled it in as noisy a catharsis as has been noted for a long time in American fiction.

The crisis is religious in one sense, though it scarcely has a basis in theological symbolism.

"A man cannot live without a focus," he says to Leverett in South Carolina. "Without some kind of faith, if you want to call it that. I didn't have any more faith than a tomcat. Nothing. Nothing! . . ." (*House*, p. 54) [28]

In this context, a lack of faith is like a lack of light and air, a secular "dark night of the Soul," of the sort described in the passage of Donne's sermon, used as the novel's epigraph. In Cass's kind of world, God will not "set this house on fire"; the initiative will have to come from Cass himself. And, while the cure seems to be complete, as he tells about it in South Carolina, there is no reason to believe that it might not break out again. It is true, however, that he has "met his match," has expelled his tormentor and killed him. More than that, he has seen the "scum" in himself and killed it; it seems to have disappeared forever over the edge of the cliff near Sambuco.

Part Two of the novel, in which Cass and Leverett "go after" the Sambuco incident together, trying to collaborate on explanations and reasons, carries as its epigraph the last stanza of Theodore Roethke's title poem of the 1953 book, *The Waking*.[29]

> *This shaking keeps me steady. I should know.*
> *What falls away is always. And is near.*
> *I wake to sleep, and take my waking slow.*
> *I learn by going where I have to go.*

These lines should give us a clue to the "peace" Cass has discovered finally. It is an uneasy peace, for "What falls away is always. And is near." Roethke's own experience, as the evidence of the poems gives it, involved a great dependence upon the father-image, a "falling away" from it, an apparent solution in marriage and in the pleasures of sex, and a crisis of "nothingness." [30] There is no doubt that in both cases the experiencing of *il niente, la nullità,* was traumatic, a major challenge to the heroic self. As the fascist *carabiniere* asks of him,

> ". . . Have you not pictured to yourself the whole horrible vista of eternity? . . . The absolute blankness, . . . stretching out for ever and ever, the pit of darkness which you are hurling yourself into, the nothingness, the void, the oblivion?" (*House*, pp. 195–96)

In one sense at least, the condition is "américaine." Cass has come from the country near Wilmington, North Carolina, on the Cape Fear River; at sixteen or seventeen he had come into the city, in the hope of finding sexual experience, and had lain with Vernelle Satterfield, whom he'd discovered near the 'bus station, selling copies of the Jehovah's Witnesses magazine for five cents apiece.

> ". . . in her little bedroom—she led me in with great piety and dignity, but that bed really *loomed*, I'll tell you—she had the goddamdest gallery of Jesuses you ever saw. . . . It was like a regular Jesus cult. It would have put some of those Italians back in the Abruzzi to shame." (*House*, p. 263)

The comic scene has its serious overtones. For Cass, a Protestant Southerner, seems always to have identified his failures with his religious backgrounds. More than that, he sees himself as forever in the role of the poor, ignorant American, trying desperately each time to "prove himself," and failing each time. In the weeks in Paris, with his Catholic wife and his Catholic children, he again suffers (this time, a serious) lapse in confidence. "You know," he tells Leverett, "the old Anglo-Saxon hellfire which we just can't ever get rid of." (p. 268) Here, trying to justify himself as a painter, he suffers from what he calls "wild Manichean dreams, dreams that told him that God was not even a lie, but worse, that He was weaker even that the evil He created and allowed to reside in the soul of man, that God Himself was doomed, and the landscape of heaven was not gold and singing but a space of terror which stretched in darkness from horizon to horizon." (pp. 275–76)

There is no doubt that the experience is similar to the Kierkegaardian *Sickness Unto Death*.[31] Cass's "cure" for it consists of wild plunges into excess: drinking, gambling, "the vices" if you will. He is more prodigiously a drunk, with a more Gant-ian appetite than ever Milton Loftis could have had. His experiences of "Nothing!" are grandly climactic, leading into agony dreams, long bouts with the

whisky bottle,[32] gambling, and whoring. He even goes the
way of the modern scientific humanist, stealing a hundred
capsules of a new medicine, which Flagg had himself
"lifted" from the P.S. in Naples, in order to help his
friend Michele. (pp. 206–10) But, of course, the act, like
others of his life, is scarcely a triumph, and certainly does
not lead to a conquest of self.

That conquest must come melodramatically. At least
Cass has an antagonist he can recognize; he survives all of
the terrors of his *nullità* because of that. Mason Flagg has
finally, in *his* excesses, provided Cass with an opportunity
to rid himself of his. "Not to believe in some salvation,"
he says later to Leverett, "to have disbelief rolled over on
top of ones head like an un-removable stone yet at times
like this . . . to see such splendour and glory writ across
the heavens & upon the quiet sand and to see all certitude
& sweetness in ones own flesh & seed scampering tireless &
timeless on the shore, and then still not believe, is something that sickens me to my heart and center. . . ."
(*House*, p. 294) [33]

The story of Cass's illness and of his own curing of it
has something of the existentialist impact of Faulkner's **A
Fable**.[34] Or, it is a dramatization of Faulkner's key phrases
in the Stockholm Address of 1950.[35] The fact is that many
great artists of the twentieth century have had visions of
this Manichaean struggle: Catholics, Protestants, and
Jews have all had some hand in portraying the agony, and
some have suggested—or imagined—a cure. *Set This
House on Fire* is notable for its having come really to grips
with the problem, and left it after a masterpiece of story-
telling; this, Faulkner, in all his earnestness, was not able
to do in *A Fable*, though he certainly managed elsewhere.
Styron's most recent novel sets the imagination agoing, in
the expectation of an American literature of existential-
ism, as Ihab Hassan has said.[36] But it is perhaps best not
to name it that, for fear of weighing it down with labels
and classification. The important fact is that Styron has
used his talents mightily and to a good effect in this novel.
The subject of both it and *Darkness* is the "Nothing!"

that both Helen and Milton Loftis cry out as he leaves her
and the grave of the girl he has killed by tenderness. It is
also Kinsolving's word; but he denies it dramatically, and
appears at the end of *House* to have found a way of
keeping it from him forever.[37]

8   CONCLUSION

REGARDLESS of the necessary limiting of my subject, I
think I can testify to the talent shown by those persons
who have survived elimination. My concern here has been
to make room for more and younger writers by avoiding
the ever-present temptation to concentrate upon the great
genius of modern Southern writing, William Faulkner.
The scholarship and criticism concerning Faulkner has
been so great that he has of necessity put any number of
worthy writers in the shade. I have wished to show how
immensely varied the scene is. Several of Faulkner's contemporaries are now beginning to receive competent
book-length studies: Katherine Anne Porter, Eudora
Welty, Carson McCullers, and Elizabeth Madox Roberts,
among them. Others will, I am sure, be studied at length
in the future. But there is a tendency still to think of
modern Southern fiction in terms of Faulkner. The writers
I have considered here comprehend a much greater variety
of literary achievement than Faulkner does. Most of them
are not confined to the analysis and elaboration of a
"postage stamp of native soil," [1] but have experimented
with varieties of landscape, place, and time. The scope of
Eudora Welty's fiction, for example, has been sufficiently
explained already. Katherine Anne Porter moves quickly
in and out of the South. In fact, many of our writers, like
William Styron, have correlated their interest in the
Southern atmosphere with more universal modern problems. With few exceptions, Southern fiction portrays the

world rather than Mississippi or Georgia. This high ambition does not necessarily make it better fiction, but it does testify to a break from the earlier generations of writers, who felt impelled the majority of times to limit themselves.

Madison Jones and Louis Rubin take up the issue, or something fairly close to it, in the panel discussion at Wesleyan College. They are discussing Styron's *Lie Down in Darkness*:

> JONES: But don't you think in *Lie Down in Darkness* that as long as he is at home, Styron makes you feel closer to the character? I mean, that last business about the girl seems to be pretty bad.
>
> RUBIN: What I think about that book is that the book takes place in a Southern city, Port Warwick—something like Newport News, but I don't feel that the family in the book are essentially what they are because of the community at all. I think this is what Mr. Styron wanted them to be. He wanted Peyton Loftis to suffer because of several generations, etc., but I don't think she does. I think it is purely because of these particular people involved. Their little private things are apart from the community, and I don't get the same sense of community even when they are writing about things in Port Warwick that you would have in a Faulkner novel.[2]

This exchange does raise a question that is not as easy to answer as the participants seemed to think. Much of the quality of Southern literature has come from *place*, and desertion of place, as in the case of Styron brings a quite different kind of fiction into being. To answer with a deliberate rejection on the grounds that to go beyond place is to lose touch with reality is an unsatisfactory approach, not only to Southern literature, but to fiction itself, as Styron has said, he does not consider himself strictly a "Southern" novelist, but experience in the South does often yield great rewards. Just what role does place have in establishing the terms of fiction? Sometimes, as in the case of a war fiction, very little indeed. The entire circumstance of a war tends to cut a swath across regions, so that the New York City boy and the Mississippi farm-boy have common experiences, and their regional differences have little to do with what they do. Styron, in both *Lie Down in Darkness* and *Set This House on Fire*, was trying to go beyond regional peculiarities. Port Warwick is, certainly middle-classville, and not especially Virginia. The return of Cass Kinsolving to rustic peace involves him in South Carolina, but Styron is not contrasting that state with postwar Europe; he is, rather, defining two major psychological and religious states of being in human nature. Kinsolving naturally, once he had purged himself of the nastiness that Mason Flagg had accentuated, shifted the scene; South Carolina became his place of retreat, but it might also have been Massachusetts or New Hampshire.

Nevertheless, place does yield undeniable values and virtues. Miss Welty's *Delta Wedding* needs to be in Mississippi; and, while many of the details of *A Curtain of Green* might apply to the lower middle class anywhere in the country, there are certain accents, particulars, peculiarities, which identify the place as Southern. Much of the time, critics (especially European critics) are inclined to assume that place in Southern fiction will automatically be "grotesque," and the clichés of reviewers, nourished by quick glances at Capote (the *early* Capote), McCullers, Welty, and O'Connor, are often used about works they don't really suggest at all. There is something unquestionably "Southern" in certain works of Andrew Lytle, Caroline Gordon, Elizabeth Madox Roberts, and Stark Young, for example.

It is often true that these and other writers do best when they deal with familiar territory. But this does *not* mean that, once they settle upon a Southern locale they are bound to write about grotesque creatures in a weird world. Capote's *The Grass Harp* is an inferior work not because it treats Southern life, and Southern life is an oversimplified, antiquated life, but rather because it is an inferior work. The tree house would have been quaint in Maine, in South Dakota, or in Oregon. Place is communicated in the special texture of a fiction when that texture is suffused by the quality—of weather, of landscape, of changes in the seasons, of the textures of leaves, mold, birds, animals, the lowering and raising of the water level, etc.—that belongs to a region. Certain things are true of Mississippi, Alabama, Georgia, and the Carolinas (and I am not thinking of sociological textures, which are a quite different matter) that are not true (or, are not true in the same degree or in the same depth) of Connecticut, Michigan, or for that matter, the western part of Texas. But I have already discussed this matter of place at some length,[3] and I think the issue is fairly obvious.

There *are* qualities in Southern fiction that depend much upon their being South; there are others that do not. Such a phenomenon as the Negro novel has a Southern point of reference, surely, but the South becomes mainly a sociological, a psychological, and a moral reference point in this case. There is a world of difference between Faulkner's or Miss Welty's or Mrs. McCullers' view of the Negro, and the Negro's view of himself (as in the case of Richard Wright's *Black Boy* and the first part of Ralph Ellison's *Invisible Man*); it is as though they were treating of vastly different kinds of being. This is because the Negro novelist is largely a *displaced* Southerner, while the Negro in the novel written by the white Southerner has a quite different life at stake. This does not necessarily make the Negro of the second kind an inferior person; he is often, as in the case of Mrs. McCullers' *The Heart Is a Lonely Hunter* and Elizabeth Spencer's *The Voice at the Back Door*, most sympathetically drawn and genuinely realized, and he is often more clearly identifiable, not in spite of but because of his being related to a region and its total community, than is the Negro at war with the world (as in Richard Wright) struggling to find an ideological source of articulation.[4]

ii

If a group of writers have produced a group of works within a certain span of time, these works should bear certain marks of similarity. What I have been discuss-

ing as place is one of these; and with it is the special
disposition to the past, to tradition, and to a special set of
events in history. Surely a climactic event like the Civil
War, which had both significant cause and basic effects, is
bound to influence the literature of the region which
suffered defeat in it. Robert Penn Warren, writing at the
beginning of the centennial observances of 1961–65,
speaks of the Civil War as "our only 'felt' history—history
lived in the national imagination. . . . It is an overwhelm-
ing image of human, and national experience." [5] He goes
on, by way of differentiating the Southern from the
Northern reaction, to say that "In defeat the Solid South
was born—not only the witless automatism of fidelity to
the Democratic Party but the mystique of prideful 'difference,' identity, and defensiveness." [6]

There is no question that the Civil War, and defeat in
it, had an impactive effect upon the South; it was like a
sledgehammer blow that pushes a post that much further
into the ground, and guarantees that it will stay firmly
implanted that much longer. But I think that the Civil
War was a literary opportunity as well; that is, Southerners became markedly more specifically a kind of group, a
kind of culture, because of it. The same may be said of the
Jews: that they developed a culture, a way of life, a "way
of putting it," a kind of humor and wit, because of their
persecutions and wanderings, and because they had to
remain a cohesive group or go mad. This particular aspect
of Southern literature is hard to assess. Shreve McCannon,
who comes from Alberta, Saskatchewan (which is just
barely south of the North Pole), needles Quentin Compson about the peculiar dispositions of the South: [7] "*Tell
about the South. What's it like there. What do they do
there. Why do they live there. Why do they live at all—*" [8]
And the novel ends with Shreve goading Quentin further:

> ". . . Now I want you to tell me just one thing more.
> Why do you hate the South?"
> "I dont hate it," Quentin said, quickly, at once, immedi-
> ately; "I dont hate it," he said. *I dont hate it* he thought,
> panting in the cold air, the iron New England dark; *I dont.
> I dont! I dont hate it! I dont hate it!*" (p. 378)

Elsewhere in Faulkner's work, the Civil War has a noticeable effect in the figure of Gail Hightower of *Light in August* (1932), paralyzed into inaction by a frenzy of memory of the alleged heroism of his grandfather; in the strange conjunction of the Civil War and World War 1 of *Sartoris* (1929); in the adventures of the young Bayard Sartoris and his Negro companion, Ringo, of *The Unvanquished* (1938).

Elsewhere in Southern literature, there are of course Andrew Lytle's *The Long Night* (1934) and the *Velvet Horn* (1957), and Stark Young's *So Red the Rose*.[9] But the influence is pervasive; as I have said in chapter one of this book, place and experience interact; in the course of decades, assuming that there is some stability, the result becomes a tradition, and it takes on the peculiarities both of where it is and what it has been. The element of guilt, the tendency of that guilt to change after a certain time (whether into clichés of automatic excuse or into a fixed sense of pride and moral burden). The effect that defeat has upon local pride and upon the ceremonials that publicly acknowledge its heroes: these are just a few of many legacies left by the major event of Southern history, this only major "felt experience" of our past.

I believe Faulkner to be the pivot of that influence upon modern literature. A "moral burden" cannot last forever. More recently writers from the South have been less concerned to show their stigmata. And it is also true that the center of the guilt has shifted, northward; as it has, the entire onus of blame, so confidently assessed by the New England abolitionists as being Southern, has also become Northern as well.[10] So that, when Styron settles upon Sambuco, Italy, for the major place of *Set This House on Fire*, he has moved away from the special moral dispositions of the Southerner looking at portraits of colonels, or addressing himself to the landscape of his youth, or to the special qualities of feudal vengeance or pride. Which does not mean that Styron has fixed target on a superior work of art; he has assumed a larger risk, moved into a far more competitive field, entered a tradition of psychological and moral analysis that has been occupied by Kierkegaard, Mann, Sartre, and Camus before him. It is a worthy step, but it is a step taken at some peril.

One observation about the writers I have discussed has to do with the remarkable skill most of them have shown in the form of the short story. Almost every one (Capote, Price, McCullers, Porter, and O'Connor conspicuously among them) has produced distinguished work in that form. And one may argue that such writers as Eudora Welty have managed pre-eminently in it.[11] The casual glance, the sketch, the practice-piece are all a part of the art of Southern fiction. Both Flannery O'Connor and Shirley Anne Grau began with short stories and novels; this practice occurred in both Hemingway's and Fitzgerald's cases; and in Faulkner's the short fiction is most impressively a *multum in parvo* reflection of the novels. All of this would be merely a statistic, were it not for the fact that the short stories have an amazing excellence. I do not and cannot imagine any better examples of the form in modern literature. Flannery O'Connor's A *Good Man Is Hard to Find,* Eudora Welty's A *Curtain of Green,* and Shirley Ann Grau's *The Black Prince* are first books of surprising maturity. They were followed by novels in each case, but no one can say that in any of them the novel proved a superior exercise.

It is hard to offer a concluding set of remarks about this group of writers. It is obvious that a tradition of writing became self-generative and that it will remain so. This does not mean that Southern fiction is or will remain superior to all others. There are, it seems to me, at least four areas of contemporary fiction that now flourish: the Southern, the Negro, the Jewish, and the War novel.[12] Each has its distinguishing cultural backgrounds, its distinctive experience, its kinds of emphasis, and its forms of literary excellence. In a few cases, the literature is still embedded in the polemic (James Baldwin, for example, tends to be a better essayist than a novelist); but this does not need to continue to be true. The history of modern American Jewish fiction is in this case exemplary. Leslie Fiedler says somewhere that the Negro saved the American Jew from the embarrassments of the ghetto life, and therefore allowed him to think and write about other matters. Like most Fiedler remarks, this one is interesting and slightly more than half true, and the truth of it relates to the conditioning of a culture as it moves from polemic to literature. Negro literature will one day come to have as much distinction as Southern literature now has; tokenism will just not prove to be enough in this area, as it turned out to be less than enough in Southern fiction beginning with about 1925. It is really a question, not of a wealth of experience (who besides the Negro is feeling more deeply and liking it less in America today?), but of its becoming freshly and increasingly available to the imagination. But a perspective is necessary; the distance from the Civil War eventually released a great flood of Southern literature. Within that war, and in the decades following it, except for a very few unimportant efforts, there was no Southern literature of the first rank. The immediate reactions to experience were the diary, the journal, the public address. These are not works of art, but the materials of art, that are picked up later and reformed.

We have had that "Southern Renaissance," and we are having it. But it is true that it becomes a matter of generations. A genius like Faulkner can take the pressures of both past and present and make of them not only a new fiction but a new method of writing as well, a complex set of literary interchanges which causes a revolution in literary style and structure. Other Southern writers, less overwhelmed by the impact of local circumstances, tend to move eventually away from them, and they create a different literature. The core of the Southern literary tradition is contained within the years 1925 and 1960; at the moment there do not appear to be any startlingly new developments, beyond those already discerned in those years. To say more than this is a bit like one's sitting on his horse's head, in order to see the landscape more clearly.

1—Definitions and Limits

1. *Renaissance in the South: A Critical History of the Literature, 1920–1960* (Chapel Hill: University of North Carolina, 1963), pp. 203–13. The book is a mine of facts, though there are too many writers considered to allow any of them much attention.

2. *Ibid.*, p. 4.

3. "The Southern Temper," in *South: Modern Southern Literature in its Cultural Setting*, edited by Louis D. Rubin, Jr. and Robert D. Jacobs (Garden City, New York: Doubleday, 1961), p. 48.

4. *Ibid.*, pp. 49–52.

5. *Ibid.*, pp. 53–54.

6. "The Historical Dimension," in *The Burden of Southern History* (New York: Vintage, 1961), p. 31. Originally published in 1960 by the Louisiana State University Press.

7. In *Death in the Afternoon* (New York: Scribner's, 1932), pp. 53–54. He was referring to certain writings of Waldo Frank.

8. I suggest the following three collections of essays: *Southern Renascence: The Literature of the Modern South*, edited by Louis D. Rubin, Jr. and Robert D. Jacobs (Baltimore: the Johns Hopkins University Press, 1953); *South* (already cited above); and *The Lasting South: Fourteen Southerners Look at Their Home* (Chicago: Regnery, 1957).

9. The pamphlet reporting the discussion, with Louis Rubin as moderator, was published at Wesleyan College.

10. She was referring here to Madison Jones, who had just

offered an analysis of the Southerner's attitude toward the Civil War.

11. See Rosa Coldfield's sentiments concerning Sutpen and the Confederate defeat, William Faulkner's *Absalom, Absalom!* (New York: Random House, 1936).

12. Thomas Wolfe, *Look Homeward, Angel* (New York: Scribner's, 1929).

13. *Delta Wedding* (New York: Harcourt Brace, 1946). See below, chap. 3, for a discussion of this novel.

14. As John L. Stewart has pointed out, in 1925 the "Renascence" had scarcely begun. See his truly distinguished book, *The Burden of Time: The Fugitives and Agrarians* (Princeton University Press, 1965), pp. 94–95.

15. See Louis D. Rubin, Jr., "The Difficulties of Being a Southern Writer Today: Or, Getting Out from under William Faulkner," *The Journal of Southern History*, 29 (November, 1963), 486–94.

16. *Let Us Now Praise Famous Men* (Boston: Houghton Mifflin, 1941), p. 246. Quoted by Peter Ohlin in *Agee* (New York: Obolensky, 1966), p. 73.

17. Stewart, p. 96. For examples of this problem in Faulkner, see especially *Absalom, Absalom!*; in Miss Porter, the "Miranda" stories, conspicuously "Old Mortality," in *Pale Horse, Pale Rider* (New York: Harcourt Brace, 1939), pp. 3–89. See below, chap. 2, for a discussion of Miss Porter's work.

18. Concerning this matter and related matters, see Tony Tanner's *The Reign of Wonder: Naivety and Reality in American Literature* (Cambridge University Press, 1965). Tanner's principal thesis is that the American artist moved more and more toward a fabric of particulars, away from abstractions, and often evaluated both literature and morality in terms of the concrete details at their command.

19. See Stewart, *op. cit.*, chap. 3, pp. 91–171, "Toward Agrarianism."

20. See Robert B. Heilman, *op. cit.*, pp. 49–51.

21. Section ii of this chapter is based upon an essay published in a special issue of the London *Times Literary Supplement*, in November of 1954; it was reprinted in *American Writing Today*, edited by Allan Angoff (New York: New York University Press, 1957), pp. 71–80. I have revised it rather drastically, and brought it up to date.

22. My first experiment in this kind of discussion was in an

essay, "The Sense of Place," published in *South, op. cit.,* pp. 60–75. I have made a number of changes and excisions, in the course of adapting it for use here.

23. The most incisive literary portrayal of this failure occurs in Allen Tate's ambitious and brilliant poem, *Ode to the Confederate Dead.* See *Poems, 1922–1947* (New York: Scribner's, 1948), pp. 19–23.

24. "Place in Fiction," *South Atlantic Quarterly,* 55 (January, 1956), 62. For a discussion of Miss Welty's fiction, see below, chap. 3.

25. See *The Collected Poems* (New York: Knopf, 1955), pp. 27–46. See also "The Paltry Nude Starts on a Spring Voyage." pp. 5–6.

26. This is hypothetically the South, a metaphor, or a point of convergence of the imaginary and the real. The actual often doesn't look different at all from the North, except perhaps in the pace of changes in weather and in the kinds and qualities of flora.

27. *The Mind of the South* (New York: Doubleday, 1954), p. 117. Originally published by Knopf in 1941.

28. *The Fathers* (New York: Putnam, 1938).

29. *Go Down, Moses* (New York: Random House, 1942), p. 193.

30. *The Great Meadow* (New York: Viking, 1930), p. 43.

31. *The Time of Man* (New York: Viking, 1945), p. 232. Originally published by Viking, 1926.

32. See below, chap. 7, for a full discussion of Styron's work.

33. *Delta Wedding, op. cit.,* p. 4.

34. Faulkner, *The Hamlet, op. cit.,* pp. 182–83.

35. *Porgy* (New York: Doram, 1925), pp. 11, 56.

36. *The View from Pompey's Head* (Garden City: Doubleday, 1954), p. 378.

37. "Emily Dickinson," in *Reactionary Essays in Poetry and Ideas* (New York: Scribner's, 1936), p. 12.

2—The Tradition of the Modern

1. Frederick P. W. McDowell's *Ellen Glasgow and the Ironic Art of Fiction* (University of Wisconsin Press, 1960) is pre-eminently the best recent book on her work; it also contains an excellent checklist of Glasgow criticism, pp. 268–80. The autobiography (called *The Woman Within*) was published by Harcourt, Brace in 1954; and a generous selec-

tion of the letters, edited by Blair Rouse, was issued by the same publisher in 1958. Of special interest is Louis D. Rubin's *No Place on Earth: Ellen Glasgow, James Branch Cabell, and Richmond-in-Virginia* (Austin: University of Texas Press, 1959), originally a supplement to *The Texas Quarterly*.

2. *Elizabeth Madox Roberts: American Novelist* (Norman: University of Oklahoma Press, 1956), p. 22. See also McDowell's *Elizabeth Madox Roberts* (New York: Twayne, 1963), a very good introductory study. Pages 170-72 contain a brief, annotated checklist of criticism. Earl H. Rovit's *Herald to Chaos: The Novels of Elizabeth Madox Roberts* (Lexington: University of Kentucky Press, 1960) demonstrates the author's usual critical acumen.

3. *The Great Meadow* (New York: Viking, 1930), p. 22. The "text" is Bishop Berkeley's *The Principles of Human Knowledge* (1710). The best study of this novel is in McDowell, pp. 85-105.

4. Contrast with Andrew Lytle's *The Long Night* (Indianapolis: Bobbs-Merrill, 1936); for a discussion of this novel, see below, chap. 5.

5. There is an embarrassment of riches here. The superlative study is John L. Stewart's *The Burden of Time: The Fugitives and Agrarians* (Princeton University Press, 1965). Yet, strangely perhaps, it is to the great credit of Louise Cowan's *The Fugitive Group: A Literary Study* (Baton Rouge: Louisiana State University Press, 1959) that Stewart's book does not supercede it, but rather works with it, the two positions supplementing each other excellently well. Two other recent studies are John Bradbury's *The Fugitives: A Critical Account* (Chapel Hill: University of North Carolina Press, 1958), which is just a bit too much affected by critical jargon; and Alexander Karanikas' *Tillers of a Myth: Southern Agrarians as Social and Literary Critics* (Madison: University of Wisconsin Press, 1966).

6. *I'll Take My Stand: The South and the Agrarian Tradition*, by Twelve Southerners (New York: Harper's, 1930); "The Briar Patch," a series of statements about the Agrarians and the Negro problem, is on pages 246-64.

7. His first publication was a biography, *John Brown: The Making of a Martyr* (New York: Payson and Clarke, 1929). Both Allen Tate and Andrew Nelson Lytle contributed biographies, in their cases, of Confederate dignitaries. Leonard Casper, in *Robert Penn Warren: The Dark and Bloody Ground* (Seattle: University of Washington Press, 1960), p.

89, says of *John Brown* that it suffers from being a compromise of fiction and fact: ". . . Warren has jeopardized the reader's earnest judgment by the use of fictional devices such as reporting the most intimate thoughts and emotions of John Brown without reference to their presumed origin in his letters and journals."

8. "The Achievement of Robert Penn Warren," *South Atlantic Quarterly*, 47 (October, 1948), 563. Stewart is especially good in his analyses of Warren. See also *The Burden of Time*, *op. cit.*, chaps. 9 and 10, pp. 427–542.

9. Last 10 lines of "The Return: An Elegy," in *Selected Poems, 1923–1943* (New York: Harcourt Brace, 1944) p. 78.

10. *God Without Thunder: An Unorthodox Defense of Orthodoxy* (New York: Harcourt Brace, 1930). See also several essays from Ransom's *The World's Body* (New York: Scribner's, 1938).

11. In its Agrarian formulation, the idea might assume this shape (Stewart's words): the child leaves an Agrarian homestead, symbol of the natural world of both good and evil, and enters an abstract realm containing neither good nor evil. (*South Atlantic Quarterly*, p. 568) There are many variants of this problem in Southern literature; John Crowe Ransom's poem, "Antique Harvesters," may be counted one of them. See *Selected Poems* (New York: Knopf, 1945), pp. 50–51.

12. This is also often held to be the "flaw" or "mistake" of Thomas Sutpen, in Faulkner's *Absalom, Absalom!* (New York: Random House, 1936).

13. *All the King's Men* (New York: Harcourt Brace, 1946). There has of course been much speculation concerning the relationship of Willie Stark to Huey Long, who was assassinated September 10, 1936. Several novels were based on his career, among them John Dos Passos' *Number One* (1943).

14. Produced at the University of Minnesota in 1946. Later another play, titled the same as the novel, appeared at The East 74th Street Theatre, October 16, 1959. This dramatic version, also done by Warren, was published by Random House in 1960.

15. It is important that the dissertation is on Southern history, the life of a certain Cass Mastern; it is also important that, at the end, Burden returns to the dissertation, with a fullness of knowledge he had not earlier had.

16. See *All the King's Men*, pp. 424–25, for the final dialogue of Burden and Stark.

17. My remarks about Miss Gordon are based upon an essay published in a special issue devoted to her work, in *Critique*, 1 (Winter, 1956), 29–35.

18. See *The Women on the Porch* (New York: Scribner's, 1944). A similar contrast occurs in *The Garden of Adonis* (New York: Scribner's, 1937).

19. The role of Allen Tate in Miss Gordon's fiction is of much interest; his point of view certainly affected her part of the way, and his personality is not infrequently drawn upon.

20. *The Women on the Porch, op. cit.*, p. 126.

21. "Portrait: Old South," in *The Days Before* (New York: Harcourt Brace, 1952), p. 155.

22. Miranda is not named specifically in this collection, though the figure and sensitivity of the Miranda character occur in at least three stories. William L. Nance, in *Katherine Anne Porter and the Art of Rejection* (Chapel Hill: University of North Carolina Press, 1964), p. 5, suggests fourteen stories in which the Miranda type is present; these include "Theft," "The Jilting of Granny Weatherall," "Hacienda," and the title story from *The Flowering Judas*.

23. Cf. Stewart's remark (*The Burden of Time, op. cit.*) about the "legendary" and the "actual" in views of the South (p. 96); he continues, saying that "for some such as Faulkner and Miss Porter this recognition [of the diversity of types of each] provided the ultimate source of many of their most intensely moving and meaningful fictions. . . ."

24. In *The Leaning Tower and Other Stories* (New York: Harcourt Brace, 1944), pp. 33–58.

25. In *Pale Horse, Pale Rider* (New York: Harcourt Brace, 1939), pp. 3–89.

26. The three sections of that story are dated 1885–1902, 1904, and 1912; the third story of *Rider*, the title story, takes place in 1917; the grandmother's time, of course, extends back into pre-Civil War days.

27. For a full series of speculations upon it, see Nance, *op. cit.*, chap. 4, pp. 80–155, and Harry J. Mooney, Jr., *The Fiction and Criticism of Katherine Anne Porter* (University of Pittsburgh Press, 1957), pp. 16–34. An excellent introduction to Miss Porter's work is George Hendrick's *Katherine Anne Porter* (New York: Twayne, 1965).

28. Nance, *op. cit.*, pp. 3–11.

29. " 'Noon Wine': The Sources," *The Yale Review*, 46 (Autumn, 1956), 24.

30. Some of my remarks about "Noon Wine" were origi-

nally given at a meeting of the College English Association in Chicago, April, 1956, and published in the *CEA Critic*, 18 (November, 1956), 1, 6–7.

31. Nance, *op. cit.*, p. 6.

32. *Ship of Fools* (Boston: Little Brown, 1962).

33. "Katherine Anne Porter Personally," in *Images of Truth: Remembrances and Criticism* (New York: Harper and Row, 1962), p. 49. There is much more; the paragraph needs to be read in its entirety.

34. "*Ship of Fools*: Notes on Style," *Four Quarters*, 12 (November, 1962), 55.

35. "*Ship of Fools* and the Critics," *Commentary*, 34 (October, 1962), 280.

3—Eudora Welty and Carson McCullers

1. *Manuscript*, 3 (June, 1936), 21–29. It was collected in *A Curtain of Green* (New York: Doubleday Doran, 1941), pp. 231–50.

2. "Place in Fiction," *Southern Atlantic Quarterly*, 55 (January, 1956), 57–72. It was subsequently published as a pamphlet by Harcourt Brace, 1957, in 300 copies.

3. The image is also used in *Delta Wedding* (New York: Harcourt Brace, 1946), p. 46.

4. See above, chap. 1, my discussion of place and the modern Southern novel.

5. "Fiction in Review," *Nation*, 157 (October 2, 1943), 386–87. Cited by Albert J. Griffith, in *Eudora Welty's Fiction*, an unpublished Ph.D. dissertation, University of Texas, 1959, pp. 109–10.

6. "Some Notes on River Country," *Harper's Bazaar*, 2786 (February, 1944), 156. Quoted by Griffith in *op. cit.*, p. 33.

7. *Ibid.*, p. 18. The Natchez Trace, featured in *The Robber Bridegroom*, appears also in several of the stories.

8. Robert Daniel, "The World of Eudora Welty," in *Southern Renascence: The Literature of the Modern South*, edited by Louis D. Rubin, Jr. and Robert J. Jacobs (Baltimore: The Johns Hopkins University Press, 1953), p. 306. Originally published in the *Hopkins Review*, 6 (Winter, 1953) 49–58.

9. "How I Write," *Virginia Quarterly Review*, 31 (Spring, 1955), 242. See also *Short Stories* (New York: Harcourt Brace, 1949).

10. "The Love and Separateness in Eudora Welty," in *Selected Essays* (New York: Random House, 1958), p. 160. This essay originally appeared in the *Kenyon Review* 6 (Spring, 1944), 246–69. It concerns the two early collections of short stories, *A Curtain of Green* and *The Wide Net, and Other Stories.*

11. See Warren, *loc. cit.*

12. First published in the *Atlantic Monthly,* 167 (April, 1941), 443–50.

13. "Clytie," in *A Curtain of Green,* pp. 155–71. Originally in *Southern Review,* 7 (Summer, 1941), 52–64.

14. In *A Curtain of Green,* pp. 231–69; originally published in *Manuscript,* 3 (June, 1936), 21–29.

15. See *The Story: A Critical Anthology* (New York: Prentice-Hall, 1950), p. 355.

16. Ruth Vande Kieft, *Eudora Welty* (New York: Twayne, 1962), pp. 38–39.

17. "*Delta Wedding* as Region and Symbol," *Sewanee Review,* 60 (Summer, 1952), 397–417. This essay, revised, was made a chapter of Hardy's *Man in the Modern Novel* (Seattle: University of Washington Press, 1964), 175–93.

18. *Ibid.,* p. 404.

19. *Eudora Welty, op. cit.,* p. 93.

20. See *Wedding,* p. 46, for the image of the china lamp.

21. See Vande Kieft, p. 104.

22. *The Golden Apples* (New York: Harcourt Brace, 1949).

23. Miss Vande Kieft calls it "the most complex and encompassing of Miss Welty's works . . ." *op. cit.,* p. 111. Her study of *Apples* (pp. 111–48) is the best so far published.

24. For the most elaborate discussions of Miss Welty's use of parallels, see H. C. Morris, "Zeus and the Golden Apples: Eudora Welty," *Perspective,* 5 (Autumn, 1952), 190–99; and "Eudora Welty's Use of Mythology," *Shenandoah,* 6 (Spring, 1955), 34–40.

25. See Ruth Vande Kieft, *op. cit.,* pp. 111–12.

26. It was separately printed by Miss Welty: Greenville, Mississippi, The Levee Press, 1948.

27. See Ruth Vande Kieft, *op. cit.* pp. 122 ff., concerning the "two sets of characters" in *Apples,* the "wanderers" and those who "serve as their foils."

28. See Oliver Evans' *The Ballad of Carson McCullers* (New York: Coward-McCann, 1966) for both biographical

information and the best critical analyses of Mrs. McCullers' works. Evans' estimate of McCullers' worth seems a bit exaggerated, however (See *Ibid.*, p. 194).

29. Issue of December, 1936. See Evans, p. 34.

30. *The Heart Is a Lonely Hunter* (Boston: Houghton Mifflin, 1940).

31. *Reflections in a Golden Eye* (Boston: Houghton Mifflin, 1941).

32. *The Ballad of the Sad Café* (Boston: Houghton Mifflin, 1951).

33. "Carson McCullers: A Map of Love," *Wisconsin Studies in Contemporary Literature*, 1 (Winter, 1960), 13. Mick Kelley and Jake Blount are from *Heart*; Berenice is the Negro cook in *The Member of the Wedding* (Boston: Houghton Mifflin 1946); and Major Penderton is from *Reflections*.

34. See Evans, pp. 195–215, for the full text of her early plan.

35. I applaud Evans' common sense in his dismissing the symbolism of Charles E. Eisinger's interpretation from *Fiction of the Forties* (University of Chicago Press, 1963), p. 247, that Singer, "because he is bisexual, combines the double function of the Virgin Mary and her Son—that, however, because he lacks omniscience, he is 'the false Virgin and the false son.' " (See Evans, p. 41, n. 5)

36. Evans, *op. cit.*, p. 70.

37. Originally published in *Harper's Bazaar*, November, 1942, then reprinted with other short stories in *The Ballad of the Sad Café* (1951). See Evans, p. 88.

38. "The Theme of Spiritual Isolation in Carson McCullers," *New World Writing*, 1 (1952), p. 304.

39. Edward Albee adapted the story to the stage, and it was produced at the Martin Beck Theatre on October 30, 1963; it ran until February, 1964. It was not a conspicuous success. Both the story and the play were published in 1963 by Atheneum.

40. "Carson McCullers: A Map of Love," p. 13.

41. *Ibid.*, pp. 14–15.

42. Evans, *op. cit.*, p. 113.

43. Mrs. McCullers attended to the dramatizing of the novel, part of the way with the help of Tennessee Williams. The play was a great success (which *The Square Root of Wonderful*, her only other essay in the drama, was not); it ran for a total of 501 performances, beginning on June 5,

1950. With Ethel Waters as Berenice. Julie Harris as Frankie, and Brandon de Wilde, it could scarcely fail. Only George Jean Nathan, "the reactionary drama critic of *Esquire*," denounced it. (See Evans, *The Ballad of Carson McCullers*, pp. 152–54)

44. *Clock Without Hands* (Boston: Houghton Mifflin, 1961).

45. Evans believes *Clock* to be next best to *Member* (see *The Ballad of Carson McCullers*, p. 186); I should put both below *The Ballad of the Sad Café*.

4—James Agee and Flannery O'Connor: The Religious Consciousness

1. Macon, Georgia, Wesleyan College, 1960, p. 11.

2. In the posthumously published volume, *Everything That Rises Must Converge* (New York: Farrar, Straus and Giroux, 1965), pp. 143–90, in which the character of Sheppard, who bears some resemblance to Rayber of *The Violent Shall Bear It Away*, tried to convince the two boys that religious beliefs just don't fit the "space age." See Walter Sullivan's excellent discussion of Miss O'Connor, in the *Hollins Critic*, 2 (September, 1965), 1–10. Sullivan says of her, that, "believing as she did in a hereafter, she did not think that can happen to a human being. I do not mean that she held life cheap, but rather that she saw it in its grandest perspective." (p. 8)

3. See John W. Hunt's *William Faulkner: Art in Theological Tension* (Syracuse University Press, 1965), pp. 20–21.

4. *Faulkner in the University*, edited by Frederick L. Gwynn and Joseph L. Blotner (Charlottesville: University of Virginia Press, 1959), p. 86. See also pp. 62–63, 68, and 117. In the last of these remarks, he says that "everyone that has had the story of Christ and the Passion as a part of his Christian background will in time draw from that. There was (in *Light in August*) no deliberate interest to repeat it. That the people to me come first. The symbolism comes second."

5. *A Death in the Family* (New York: McDowell Obolensky, 1957); Tad Mosel dramatized the novel, and it was produced at the Belasco Theatre in New York, November 30, 1960; the play was published by Obolensky in 1961.

6. This is a fact that Leslie Fiedler does not account for in his review. He refers to it as the result of a confusion between

the limits of the novella and the ambitions of a thick family saga. See "Encounter with Death," *New Republic*, 137 (December 9, 1957), 25. Of course, one does not know what Agee would eventually have intended. Peter Ohlin, in his *Agee* (New York: Obolensky, 1966), p. 2, speaks of two recently discovered new chapters of *Death*.

7. Dwight Macdonald, "Death of a Poet," *New Yorker*, 33 (November 6, 1957), 209–10.

8. *The Morning Watch* (Boston: Houghton Mifflin, 1951). For a study of the Christ imagery, see John S. Phillipson, "Character, Theme, and Symbol in *The Morning Watch*," *Western Humanities Review*, 15 (Autumn, 1961), 359–67.

9. His surname is never given.

10. Like Rufus' of *Death*, Richard's father had died when the boy was six years old. The thought of a death in a family was with Agee through most of his life.

11. Flannery O'Connor, "The Role of the Catholic Novelist," *Greyfriar (Siena Studies in Literature)*, 7 (1964), 8. When Miss O'Connor died, August 3, 1964, she received many tributes. Not the least of these was the Winter, 1964, issue of *Esprit* (Vol. 8, No. 1), taken over by notes and memoirs. It includes 49 statements from writers, educators, and friends. (See pp. 12–49)

12. See Sister M. Bernetta Quinn, "View from a Rock: The Fiction of Flannery O'Connor and J. F. Powers," *Critique*, 2 (Fall, 1958), 19–27: ". . . The center of all Catholic fiction is the Redemption. However mean or miserable or degraded human life may seem to the natural gaze, it must never be forgotten that God considered it valuable enough to send His only son that he might reclaim it . . ." (p. 21) See *A Handbook of Christian Theology* (New York: Meridian Books, 1958), p. 296: "Thus the God who ransoms, redeems, and delivers Israel out of her bondage is the God who, in Christ, pays the price which restores sinful mankind to freedom and new life. In this act of redemption two interrelated theological emphases are dominant: God's *love* by which He takes the initiative, and man's sin which occasions the situation from which God redeems him." Since my writing of this chapter, two essays have appeared on the subject of Flannery O'Connor's use of the Christ figure in her work: Robert Drake's " 'The Bleeding Stinking Mad Shadow of Jesus' in the Fiction of Flannery O'Connor," *Comparative Literature*

Studies, 3 (1966), 186–96; and Robert Detweiler's "The Curse of Christ in Flannery O'Connor's Fiction," in *Ibid.,* 235–45. In another version, my own remarks appeared as "The Search for Redemption: Flannery O'Connor's Fiction," in *The Added Dimension: Essays on Flannery O'Connor,* edited by Melvin J. Friedman and Lewis A. Lawson (New York: Fordham University Press, 1966), pp. 31–48.

13. "The Role of the Catholic Novelist," pp. 10–11.

14. *Ibid.,* p. 11.

15. See Melvin J. Friedman, in *Recent American Fiction,* edited by Joseph J. Waldmeir (Boston: Houghton Mifflin, 1963), p. 241. Friedman also cites Nathanael West, as does John Hawkes in the *Sewanee Review,* 70 (Summer, 1962), 396. Hawkes mentions an interesting conjunction of influences on himself: ". . . it was Melville's granddaughter [Eleanor Melville Metcalf], a lady I was privileged to know in Cambridge, Massachusetts, who first urged me to read the fiction of Flannery O'Connor, and—further—since this experience occurred just at the time I had discovered the short novels of Nathanael West."

16. *A Good Man Is Hard to Find* (New York: Harcourt Brace, 1955), p. 26.

17. *Systematic Theology* (University of Chicago Press, 1951), II, 98. It is interesting that many of Miss O'Connor's characters want to "see a sign": that is, they want Christ's divinity manifested directly. The Misfit is such a one; Hazel Motes of *Wise Blood* (New York: Harcourt Brace, 1952) struggles against a Christian mission on the grounds that Christ as God has never revealed Himself; Mr. Head and his grandson have a remarkable experience of illumination, when they see the plaster statue of a Negro (in "The Artificial Nigger," *Man,* pp. 127–28); and the young Tarwater of *The Violent Bear It Away* (New York: Farrar, Straus and Cudahy, 1960) has a "voice" (variously called "stranger," "friend," and "mentor") who tries to deny Jesus because there has been so "sign" of Him.

18. The imagery of fire in *The Violent Bear It Away* is especially ambiguous; perhaps it is a "resourceful ambiguity." At the beginning, the young Tarwater sets fire to the cabin which he thinks has the body of his great-uncle; this latter has urged him to bury him, but the boy's inner voice advises him to forget all that nonsense. When he is riding toward the city, Tarwater momentarily confuses the lights with the fire he has

just set. But, in Part Three of the novel, fire seems to have become a source of illumination as well as a means of triumphing over the devil, by burning him out.

19. *Wise Blood*, p. 19.

20. See both Friedman and Hawkes, *op. cit.* By way of distinction from *Miss Lonelyhearts*, *Wise Blood* has its hero almost reach the Christ. After Hazel Motes begins his atonement by blinding himself, and shortly following his death, his landlady sees into his eyes and through them to that "dark tunnel" which is apparently the illumination of Christ. Motes ambiguously becomes the *way* to the light and the light itself: "She sat staring with her eyes shut, into his eyes, and felt as if she had finally got the beginning of something she couldn't begin, and she saw him moving farther and farther away, farther into the darkness until he was the pin point of light." (p. 232)

21. See also page 105: "I'm going to preach there was no Fall because there was nothing to fall from and no Redemption because there was no Fall and no Judgment because there wasn't the first two. Nothing matters but that Jesus was a liar."

22. See page 191: "He wanted to be the young man of the future, like the ones in the insurance ads. He wanted, some day, to see a line of people waiting to shake his hand."

23. "Flannery O'Connor's Devil," p. 396.

24. See *A Good Man Is Hard to Find*, p. 28.

25. See Sumner J. Ferris, "The Outside and the Inside," *Critique*, 3 (Winter–Spring, 1960), 11–19. He suggests two interpretations: "that of the believer and that of the unbeliever, the violent and the passive, the saved and the damned." (p. 15) Miss O'Connor uses the Douai version of Matthew XI:12. The sense in which she probably wishes to use the quotation is indicated at the very end of the novel: the young Tarwater "felt his hunger no longer as a pain but as a tide. He felt it rising in himself through time and darkness, rising through the centuries, and he knew that it rose in a line of men whose lives were chosen to sustain it, who would wander in the world, strangers from that violent country where the silence is never broken except to shout the truth." *Violent Bear It Away*, p. 242.

26. See Miss O'Connor's own remarks at the College of Saint Teresa, quoted above. That Rayber is at times very close himself to the "madness of love" is suggested again and again.

He thinks of an "affliction" a "madness," which affects the entire family: "It lay hidden in the line of blood that touched them, flowing from some ancient source. . . . Those it touched were condemned to fight it constantly or be ruled by it." (p. 114). It is true that Rayber is more frequently than not the subject of comic treatment; also, he suffers from "*une malaise rationaliste*," as when he is described as undergoing "what amounts to a rigid ascetic discipline." (p. 114) This is a secularized version of the regimen of the saint; applied to Rayber, it tends to give him a comical and even a ludicrous aspect, but actually it indicates how close he is to the "madness" of the elder Tarwater and how easy it might have been for him to become another version of the prophet. This fact his young nephew recognizes when he tells Rayber that "the seed" had fallen "deep" in him: "It ain't a thing you can do about it. It fell on bad ground but it fell in deep." (p. 192)

27. "The Fiction Writer and His Country," in *The Living Novel: A Symposium*, edited by Granville Hicks (New York: Macmillan, 1957), pp. 162–63.

5—The Mark of Time:
Society and History in Southern Fiction

1. Andrew Lytle, "The Hind Tit," in *I'll Take My Stand*, p. 202.

2. *The Pavilion: Of People and Times Remembered, of Stories and Places* (New York: Scribner's, 1951), p. 112. Young also contributed to *I'll Take My Stand*; see "Not in Memoriam, but in Defense," p. 328–59.

3. *After Strange Gods: A Primer of Modern Heresy* (New York: Harcourt Brace, 1934), p. 18.

4. *I'll Take My Stand*, p. 328.

5. "What Is a Traditional Society?" in *Reason in Madness* (New York: Putnam's, 1941), pp. 228–29.

6. See Donald Davidson, "A Mirror for Artists," in *I'll Take My Stand*, pp. 28–60.

7. "Forms and Citizens," in *The World's Body* (New York: Scribner's, 1938), p. 30.

8. *The Fathers* (New York: Putnam's, 1938).

9. John Stewart suggests that Major Lewis Buchan "may have been partly modeled on Tate's great-grandfather, Major Lewis Bogan, of Fairfax County, Virginia, whose portrait is referred to in Tate's poem, 'The Oath'" (*The Burden of*

Time: The Fugitives and Agrarians (Princeton University Press, 1965), p. 336).

10. *The Burden of Time*, p. 337.

11. "The Working Novelist and the Mythmaking Process," *Daedalus*, 88 (Spring, 1959), 326–38; the quotations are from pp. 326, 328, and 330.

12. *The Long Night* (Indianapolis: Bobbs-Merrill, 1936), Preface.

13. "The Working Novelist and the Mythmaking Process," p. 331.

14. Brewster Ghiselin, "Trial of Light," *Sewanee Review*, 65 (Autumn, 1957) p. 29.

15. *The Velvet Horn* (New York: McDowell and Obolensky, 1957), p. 29.

16. William Humphrey, *Home from the Hill* (New York: Knopf, 1958).

17. *The Ordways* (New York: Knopf, 1965), p. 10.

18. As if by way of editorial digression, Humphrey enters a disquisition on the Southerner's link to the past: "The past lives in us. . . . For it is this, not any fixation on the Civil War, but this feeling of identity with his dead (who are the past) which characterizes and explains the Southerner . . ." (p. 36) And, later, "The Southerner is like those ancient Hebrews who preserved and recounted and gloried in the stories of double-dealing and the bloody-mindedness of their untrammeled forebears." (p. 39).

19. There are many echoes of Faulkner, in style and idea.

20. Dave Hickey, "Ostensibly a Book Review of Two Books, but too Ostentatious to Be." *Riata* (Spring, 1965), p. 57.

21. *The Black Prince and Other Stories* (New York: Knopf, 1955).

22. *The House on Coliseum Street* (New York: Knopf, 1961), p. 230.

23. *The Keepers of the House* (New York: Knopf, 1964).

24. These are "all the daughters of musick shall be brought low" and "The grasshopper shall be a burden." Ecclesiastes was also, as we all know, an important source for Hemingway. See Eccles. 1:4–5.

25. She finds the narrative point of view difficult to manage; and there are *longueurs*.

26. See Faulkner, *Go Down, Moses* (New York: Random House, 1942) pp. 262–74.

27. Walter Sullivan, *The Long, Long Love* (New York: Holt, 1959).

28. *Black Boy* (New York: Harper's, 1945).

29. See *Invisible Man* (New York: Random House, 1952), and the long excerpt from his forthcoming novel, in *The Noble Savage*, No. 1 (February, 1960), 5–49.

30. In *Intruder in the Dust* (New York: Random House, 1948).

31. *The Voice at the Back Door* (New York: McGraw-Hill, 1956). I am aware of the fact that Miss Spencer turned away from this subject, and began publishing instead, in 1960, slender volumes concerned with Americans in Europe. See *The Light in the Piazza* (New York: McGraw-Hill, 1960), a story of the desperate problems of an American woman, who is faced with the prospect of her retarded daughter's love for an Italian; and *Knights and Dragons* (New York: McGraw-Hill, 1965), set in Rome and concerned with the difficulties of a married woman whose marriage is fading and who is trying to rescue her personality from it.

6—Varieties of Fantasy

1. "Substance and Shadow," *New Yorker*, 38 (April 7, 1962), 177.

2. "Acute Particularity," *Christian Century*, 79 (June 27, 1962), 810.

3. *Delta Wedding* (New York: Harcourt Brace, 1946), p. 4.

4. "A Still Moment," in *The Wide Net, and Other Stories*, p. 88.

5. In *A Curtain of Green* (New York: Doubleday Doran, 1941), pp. 73–84.

6. In Flannery O'Connor, *A Good Man Is Hard to Find* (New York: Harcourt Brace, 1955), pp. 127–28.

7. *Radical Innocence: Studies in the Contemporary American Novel* (Princeton University Press, 1961), p. 207.

8. *Winesburg, Ohio* (New York: Modern Library, n.d.), pp. 1–5. Originally published by Huebsch in 1919.

9. As are the young Tarwater and Rayber, in *The Violent Bear It Away*. See above, chap. 4.

10. *Other Voices, Other Rooms* (New York: Random House, 1948).

11. Richard Chase, *The American Novel and Its Tradition* (New York: Anchor Books, 1957), pp. vii–xii.

12. See *Absalom, Absalom!* (New York: Random House, 1936), pp. 7–30.

13. I consider this and *The Grass Harp* (New York: Random House, 1951) as representing a distinctive period, supplemented by some of the stories in *A Tree of Night* (New York: Random House, 1949); these works are his contribution to Southern fiction as I have seen it; other books are journalistic prose (of a high order indeed) and, in the most recent case, an attempt to write a "non-fictional novel" (*In Cold Blood*, New York, Random House, 1965).

14. "*Other Voices, Other Rooms*: Oedipus between the Covers," *American Imago* (1962), 361–73.

15. Alberto Moravia, in his review of the book, thought he *was* a woman. See "Two American Writers," *Sewanee Review*, 68 (Summer, 1960), 479.

16. *Radical Innocence, op. cit.*, p. 245.

17. See Paul Levine, "Truman Capote: The Revelation of the Broken Image," *Virginia Quarterly*, 34 (Autumn, 1958), 600–617.

18. Thomas Mann, *Confessions of Felix Krull, Confidence Man*, translated by Denver Lindley (New York: Knopf, 1955).

19. Some of the stories in *A Tree of Night* ought not to go unnoticed, especially "Master Misery" (pp. 9–30 of the Signet Book edition), in which a lovely typist in New York (hating its "anonymity, its virtuous terror") sells her dreams to a strange character called Master Misery.

20. Born in East Texas in 1918, Goyen attended Rice University. *The House of Breath* (New York: Random House, 1950) is his best known work; there are several others.

21. *In a Farther Country* (New York: Random House, 1955).

22. The "Far Country" is probably Spain, but the southwest of the United States is a satisfactory newer version of it.

23. In *Ghost and Flesh: Stories and Tales* (New York: Random House, 1952), pp. 3–23.

24. *The Moviegoer* (New York: Knopf, 1961; edition used: Popular Library, 1962), which won the National Book Award in 1962; and *The Last Gentleman* (New York: Farrar Straus and Giroux, 1966). Percy was born in Birmingham, Alabama, in 1916, received a Doctor of Medicine degree from

Columbia University in 1941, and has written philosophical and medical essays in addition to his fiction.

25. *A Long and Happy Life* (New York: Atheneum, 1962); *The Names and Faces of Heroes* (New York: Atheneum, 1963); *A Generous Man* (New York: Atheneum, 1966).

26. It was almost uniformly praised upon its appearance. See Julian Mitchell, "Landscape into Art," *Spectator*, 208, 6978 (March 23, 1962), 376–77: *Life*, he says, "is, in fact, something more than 'very good.' " Robert Taubman, in *New Statesman*, 63 (March 3, 1963), 419–20, says that *Life* "shows a real talent for sympathetic observation, but suffers from its very conscious art . . ." Catharine Hughes, in *Commonweal*, 76 (April 13, 1962) 124–25, hails *Life* as "a novel which deserves all its pre-publication accolades." The usual "first novel" tributes are frequent, as they are (as nearly as I can determine) sincere.

27. See "Mantle of Faulkner?" *New Republic*, 154 (May 14, 1966) 31–33.

7—William Styron: The Metaphysical Hurt

1. Interview conducted by Peter Matthiessen and George Plimpton, for *Paris Review*, reprinted in *Writers at Work*, edited by Malcolm Cowley (New York: Viking, 1958), 273.

2. For what it is worth, I give a partial list of the speculations on Styron's "Southernness": John Aldridge, in the *New York Times Book Review*, September 5, 1951, p. 5; Malcolm Cowley, "The Faulkner Pattern," *New Republic*, 125 (October 8, 1951), 19–20 (Both of these strongly emphasize the Southern tradition); Elizabeth Janeway, in *New Leader*, 35 (January 21, 1952), 25 (she cries "Nonsense" to the idea that *Lie Down in Darkness* is a story, fable, what have you, of decadence in a Southern family); and Harvey Swados, "First Novel," *Nation* 273 (November, 1951), 453 (who criticizes Styron for "investing his corrupt family with significances").

3. As in *The Long March* (New York: Random House, 1952).

4. The *Paris Review*, 1 (Spring, 1953), 13.

5. They, and other matters emphasized by Styron, point to William Faulkner's Nobel Award Speech in 1950. Styron was, of course, powerfully influenced by Faulkner, but has managed, I think, to bring the influence under control. He once

said to David Dempsey, about *Lie Down in Darkness*: "Faulkner's [influence] was the hardest to shake off. The early parts of my novel were so imbued with his style that I had to go back and rewrite them completely. . . ." *New York Times Book Review*, September 9, 1951, p. 27.

6. *Set This House on Fire* (New York: Random House, 1960). See also his remark, in the interview published in *Writers at Work*: events like Hiroshima, he said, "don't alter one bit a writer's fundamental problems, which are Love, Requited and Unrequited, Insult, et cetera." (p. 281).

7. *Life*, 53 (July 20, 1962), 39–42. Faulkner, of course, used this square repeatedly and gave a "mythical history" of almost every timber and brick, in the long expository passages of *Requiem for a Nun* (1951).

8. In *One and Twenty* (Duke University Press, 1945), pp. 266–80.

9. "The Death-in-Life of Benjamin Reid," *Esquire*, 58 (November, 1962), 142.

10. It is not Styron's first novel, but his second, in time of publication (1952). But it must be considered a minor work.

11. See Michel Butor's "Préface" to *La Proie des flammes*, French translation (by Maurice Coindreau) of *Set This House on Fire* (Paris: Gallimard, 1962), a very interesting series of suggestions concerning the quotation from Sophocles.

12. The style used in describing Mannix generally reminds one of Faulkner's Labove, of *The Hamlet*. The characteristic attitude of deep, almost obsessive concentration, is not unusual in Faulkner's novels. But of course, Faulkner does more than *say* his character is deeply moved; the *style* communicates the madness.

13. New York and Indianapolis: Bobbs-Merrill, 1951.

14. There are two children, but the cripple, Maudie, starts few speculations and is surely an awkwardly simple "companion" of Helen Loftis' too narrow and too dry Protestantism.

15. The setting of *Darkness*, as well as the birthplace of Peter Leverett, narrator of *Set This House on Fire*. It is probably based upon Newport News, Virginia, a port city where Styron was born in 1925.

16. See the *New Leader*, 35 (January 21, 1952), p. 25.

17. This monologue is perhaps one of the most obvious borrowings from Faulkner, specifically from Part Two of *The Sound and the Fury*, an interior monologue which leads to a

suicide, which must therefore have been communicated to us from death. But Styron offers us his quite original version of the situation; the resemblance is by no means unflattering to him.

18. The Negro revival, with "Daddy Faith" presiding and Ella Swan attending with her daughter, La Ruth, is once again an "echo" of Faulkner, this time of Part Four of *The Sound and the Fury*, the celebration of Easter in the Negro church, with the Reverend Shegog, a visiting preacher from Saint Louis, officiating. Styron gains an easy contrast by inserting the evangelical event on the edges of the cemetery, and the effects are not nearly so felicitous as those in Faulkner's novels.

19. *New York Times Book Review*, September 9, 1951, p. 27.

20. Epigraph to *House*, n. p. Note that the title of *Darkness*, which must have been a commonplace metaphor of death, is also found here: "then this soule cannot be a smoake, a vapour, nor a bubble, but must lie down in darknesse, as long as the Lord of light is light it selfe . . ."

21. There have been other speculations: Michel Butor's "Préface" to the French translation says much about Sophocles' play, *Oedipus at Colonus* (see pp. xi, xviii), as does André Bonnichon, in "William Styron et le Second Oedipe," *Etudes*, 315 (October, 1962), 102. This association is of course given encouragement through Styron's having Cass Kinsolving quote from the play (see *House*, pp. 117–18). One American critic links Styron's thought with that of Sören Kierkegaard's *The Sickness unto Death*, and quotes the text to prove it (See "Cass Kinsolving: Kierkegaardian Man of Despair," *Wisconsin Studies in Contemporary Literature*, 3, 1962, 54–66). Another suggests an obscure seventeenth-century document, Henri Estienne's, translated by Richard Carew as *A World of Wonders* (Jerry A. Bryant in *South Atlantic Quarterly*, 62, 1963, 539–50). John Howard Lawson blames Styron for what he regards as the failure of *House* on his inadequate social perception, his having used Freud to set aside Marx (See *Mainstream*, 13 [October, 1960], 9–18). These interpretations having varying usefulness. The wonder is that there are so many, but it seems more sensible to note that Styron's approach to life is more "universal" than ideological or regional.

22. Leverett has, inevitably, raised questions of the in-

fluence of F. Scott Fitzgerald's Nick Carraway of *The Great Gatsby* (1925). But Leverett is not nearly so well sketched in as Carraway, and Kinsolving is surely no Gatsby. The *idea* of having a narrator, like Conrad's Marlow, question and probe at the same time as he narrates, is of course there; and there is a rough similarity of Part Two to the last section of Faulkner's *Absalom! Absalom!* (1936), where Shreve McCannon and Quentin Compson try together to reconstruct the legend of Thomas Sutpen.

23. Nick Carraway of *The Great Gatsby* remembers, in the noise of a crucial encounter on a hot July afternoon in 1922 at the Savoy Plaza Hotel, that he has just reached the age of thirty. The fact meant much more to Fitzgerald than it does to Styron.

24. "Préface," to *La Proie des flammes*, p. xi.

25. At one point Flagg points out, to Leverett, the difference between third-rate lying "and a jazzy kind of bullshit extravaganza, . . . meant with no malice at all, but only with the intent to edify and entertain." (*House*, p. 172) This remark has to do with his legendary war experiences in Yugoslavia as an agent behind the lines; he had actually been a draft dodger.

26. Butor, *op. cit.*

27. New York: Scribner's, 1925, p. 7.

28. This is the same "Nothing!" that afflicted both Milton and Helen Loftis in *Darkness*.

29. New York: Doubleday, 1953, p. 120.

30. See my essay, "Theodore Roethke: The Poetic Shape of Death," in *Theodore Roethke: A Tribute*, edited by Arnold Stein (Seattle: University of Washington Press, 1965), pp. 94–114.

31. See Lewis Lawson, *op. cit.*

32. As Leverett says, seeing him at his worst in Sambuco: "Something held him in torment and in great and desperate need: I never saw anyone I wanted so to get sober." (*House*, p. 201).

33. Here Styron indulges in one of his uncommon "Agrarian" attacks upon the North: "I should have been brought up north in N. Y. suburbs Scarsdale or somewhere on that order, where I might never have learned the quality of desire or thirst or yearning & would have ended up on Madison Ave. designing deodorant jars, with no knowledge or comprehension of the freezing solitude of the bereft and prodigal son. . . ." (*House*, p. 294).

34. New York: Random House, 1954.

35. See *William Faulkner: Three Decades of Criticism,* edited by F. J. Hoffman and Olga W. Vickery (Michigan State University Press, 1960), pp. 347–48.

36. "The Character of Post-War Fiction in America," *English Journal,* 51 (January, 1962), 7.

37. A translation of this essay on Styron appeared in *La Configuration Critique de William Styron,* edited by Melvin J. Friedman (Paris: J. J. Minard, 1967). There have been some minor revisions for publication in this place.

8—Conclusion

1. William Faulkner, Interview with Jean Stein, in *William Faulkner: Three Decades of Criticism,* p. 82.

2. "Recent Southern Fiction," Wesleyan College, 1960, p. 9.

3. See above, chap. 1.

4. This matter of the Negro *in* the South and *in* the Southern novel has not been adequately discussed. Contemporary Negroes are so much the activists that they cannot identify themselves with a community, or they do not wish to. As a result, any work (like Faulkner's *Intruder in the Dust,* 1948) which explores the Negro issue as the Negro asserting his individual manhood is considered old-fashioned. Such novelists as James Baldwin (whose tenure in the South is of very short duration indeed) conceive of the relationship with the White as a moral challenge to the White. This is also what Faulkner thinks, but the positions of the two are virtually irreconcilable.

5. *The Legacy of the Civil War: Meditations on the Centennial* (New York: Random House, 1961), p. 4.

6. *Ibid.,* p. 14. See also his novel, *Wilderness* (New York: Random House, 1961).

7. See C. Vann Woodward, *The Burden of Southern History,* especially chaps. 1, 2, and 8. See also, Allen Tate's essay, "The Profession of Letters in the South," in *The Man of Letters in The Modern World: Selected Essays, 1928–1955* (New York: 1955), pp. 305–20. Originally published in *Reactionary Essays in Poetry and Ideas* (New York: Scribner's, 1935), pp. 145–66.

8. *Absalom, Absalom!* (New York: Random House, 1936), p. 174.

9. *So Red the Rose* (New York: Scribner's, 1934). See

also Shelby Foote's novel *Shiloh* (New York: Dial, 1952), a fictionalized account of the battle.

10. See Edmund Wilson's strangely brilliant book, *Patriotic Gore: Studies in the Literature of the American Civil War* (New York: Oxford University Press, 1962).

11. I shall want here to pay a special tribute to the work of Peter Taylor. With the exception of *A Woman of Means* (New York: Harcourt Brace, 1950), a short novel of great brilliance, all of his work in fiction has been in the form of the short story. *A Long Fourth and Other Stories* (New York: Harcourt Brace, 1948), and *Happy Families Are All Alike* (New York: McDowell and Obolensky, 1959) are the two collections. The second takes its title from Tolstoi's *Anna Karenina:* "Happy families are all alike; every unhappy family is unhappy in its own way." Which of course makes for the substance of literature, all literature that's not pageantry at least.

12. See my *The Modern Novel in America* (Chicago: Regnery, 1964), Appendix One, pp. 226–55, for a discussion of all of these types.